It was *never* about a hot dog and a Coke!

A personal account of the 1960 sit-in demonstrations in Jacksonville, Florida and Ax Handle Saturday

Rodney L. Hurst Sr.

WingSpan Press

Printed in the United States of America

Published by WingSpan Press, Livermore, CA
www.wingspanpress.com

The WingSpan name, logo and colophon are the trademarks of WingSpan Publishing.

ISBN 978-1-59594-195-4
First edition 2008

Library of Congress Control Number 2007939346

Book cover design and photo imaging by Terra Herzberger.

Acknowledgments

Many persons, both living and deceased, provided the motivation for this book. I sincerely thank them for their help, support, encouragement, memories, and, above all, for their prayers, and their inspiration:

The late Rutledge Henry Pearson, my early mentor, friend, big brother, a real hero of the civil rights movement, whose dynamic leadership made so much possible.

Mary Ann Pearson, Mr. Pearson's wife, who put up with us during those sit-in years and continues excellently to represent the legacy.

Patricia Pearson, their daughter, a civil rights pioneer in her own right, who knows firsthand what school integration is all about.

The late Earl M. Johnson, our Thurgood Marshall, or was Thurgood Marshall history's Earl Johnson?

Janet Johnson, Earl's wife and my favorite non-lawyer.

Fellow author Marsha Dean Phelts, who more than anyone encouraged me to "just write the book" and who continually reminded me it needed to be written.

Former State Senator Arnett E. Girardeau, another courageous unsung civil rights pioneer and a Black pioneer in Florida politics.

The late Clanzel T. Brown, who, like Mr. Pearson, died much too early, but made his mark on the human rights scene of Jacksonville as a pioneering Urban League Executive Director.

Rev. Rudolph W. McKissick Sr., my pastor, who is always there with resolute strength, and words of spiritual direction and encouragement.

Rev. Rudolph McKissick Jr., also my pastor, cut from the same exquisite cloth of his father, and a premier spiritual voice in the country.

C. Ronald "Ronnie" Belton, a real Urban Leaguer, a civil rights activist, and President and CEO of River Place Analytics LLC. for his consistent encouragement and support; Mathis "Plute" Daniel, who, as a segregation-era Black athlete, never received a real look as a Major League baseball player; Professor Howard Denson, of Florida Community College at Jacksonville and Intelligent Eye Inc, for his keen insight, confidence, and professional editing eye; Bruce Bortz, for his outstanding excellence; Sharon Timmons and Lydia Monroe, both good friends, who knew what to look for and how to read subjective work objectively; Richard McKissick, for his knowledge of community and his longevity; Weldon Coffey Sr., who knows and remembers the Black community sports scene from the '50s until today; and R. K., a real Boomerang.

And especially my family: Ann, my wife of 41 years, who motivates and inspires me, and understood this quest to write for history; my mother, Janelle "Jan" Wilson, who feared for my personal safety during those days but nonetheless supported me, and who gave me a flair for writing—her recent illness and death, unfortunately, did not allow her to realize that this book has been written; my grandmother, Lizzie Williams, who taught me more about faith in God and the courage of your convictions than anyone; my oldest son, Rodney, who understood at an early age what the struggle is all about; my daughter-in-law Danita, who is a Godsend; my wonderful granddaughters, Marquiette and Jasmine, who know how to encourage "Granddaddy"; my youngest son, Todd, who is supportive in his own way; my sister, Joan Saunders Whitlock, who not only encouraged me to write the book, but tried to tell me how to write it; the South Carolina chapter of the family, where so much began—my cousins, Connie Foreman Daniels, Connie's husband, Dr. Barry Daniels, Milfred Foreman, Milfred's wife Stephanie, and Milfred and Connie's mother, Sally Bradley Foreman, my grand uncle Frank Foreman's widow; my brother-in-law, Robert Albertie; my late sister-in-law Brenda Albertie Priestly, and my late brother-in-law Frank Priestly, both lifelong NAACP'ers; and my gifted and talented nieces and nephews, all who keep me actively inspired and motivated: Brenda Priestly-Jackson (D'Andre),Tami Williams, D'Wayne Priestly (Cynthia), Timothy Whitlock, DeLando Williams and Cassius Priestly,—and also to Cheryl Coffey, my very supportive "other wife" (family joke). Special thanks to Terra Herzberger for her technical help with photos and newspaper clippings; and to Mrs. Camilla Thompson; Colleen Seale of the University of Florida Library; Eileen Brady of the University of North Florida Library; and Pat Morrison of the Jacksonville Public Library, for their research help.

Special thanks to Corrine Brown, Betty Holzendorf, E. Denise Lee, Tony Hill, Lydia Stewart, and Isaiah Rumlin - just because.

It was never about a hot dog and a Coke!

Very special thanks to my church families at West Friendship Baptist Church, St. Gabriel's Episcopal Church, and Bethel Baptist Institutional Church for their love and prayers.

Finally, "high fives" to Vincent Myrick, Willie McCullough, Earl Sims, Ervin Norman, Willard A. Payne, John Monroe, and Alvin G. White for their support and many years of friendship.

I thank God for the real heroes of the sit-in movement in Jacksonville—the courageous members of the Jacksonville Youth Council NAACP, living and deceased.

I praise God for His Grace, His Love, and His Gifts to me of writing, physical strength, and perseverance.

This book is dedicated
to the memory of my Mother, Janelle Saunders Wilson and
my Grandmother, Lizzie Foreman Williams

and

to the legacy and spirit of Rutledge Henry Pearson

Introduction

History has not been kind to those who forget or ignore their own history or rely on others to portray that history. Mr. Hurst has authored a gripping and informative narrative of the people and events that forged the civil rights movement in Jacksonville, Florida. His book has value in an undeveloped area as an enlightening account of events that forever changed the face of Jacksonville. It is a narrative that can be replicated throughout the south. In all too many instances, the instigators and facilitators of change have been ignored or written out of the history books, and future generations are left to conclude that change simply rolled in on the wheels of inevitability. This was clearly not the case as evidenced by Mr. Hurst's firsthand account of the turbulent and violent period when Jacksonville, and much of the south, was forced to divorce itself from a despicable and shameful history of race relations. His book can be used as a valuable resource for understanding that transformation. The typical response to racial violence in America has been to simply ignore America's bitter racial divide. Mr. Hurst's attractive and copiously illustrated book does not allow us this luxury. His simple and straightforward account speaks for itself.

Justice Leander Shaw
Florida State Supreme Court (Retired)

Foreword

I want to share with you a facet of Jacksonville's history very few are willing to discuss, let alone embrace. Although its darkness may give Jacksonville's reputation a black eye, the eye-opening details, when synthesized, provide a remarkable history worth telling.

It never ceases to amaze me how selective our memories are when it comes to situations filled with embarrassment, shame, and hurt. We choose to forget turbulent times rather than learn from them, as if not talking about them will make them go away. Just as closing our eyes does not cause us to go blind, shutting our mouths does nothing to erase memories or make events disappear from history.

Unfortunately, many whites and Blacks in Jacksonville, Florida have yet to grasp that reality. They have rationalized away the days of racism and segregation while insisting they stay buried in the past. On the surface, "Let bygones be bygones," sounds plausible. But U.S. philosopher and poet George Santanyana (1863-1952) said those "who cannot remember the past are condemned to repeat it." To paraphrase his words, those who do not learn about their past will assuredly repeat it.

The civil rights movement in the late fifties and early sixties is a history of brave and unselfish Black leaders fighting against racism and segregation, and for the equality of all people in the United States.

Most Black and white citizens of Selma, Birmingham, Memphis, Montgomery, and Atlanta are acutely familiar with the violent civil rights struggles that occurred in their cities. Though the struggles in those cities may be more familiar, Jacksonville was not immune to the same type of cruelties.

Some books about Jacksonville's civil rights history have the Student Non-Violent Coordinating Committee (SNCC) helping to organize the sit-in demonstrations in Jacksonville. One author wrote that events such as Ax-Handle Saturday legitimized Jacksonville as a progressive southern city. What a regrettably untrue statement!

It seems as if everyone in Jacksonville had a sit-in demonstration story to tell, well intentioned or not, in these books. Unfortunately, many of their accounts, plain and simply, are not true. They inaccurately present information, misread and misinterpret the time frame of many of Jacksonville's civil rights events, and quote individuals who were uninformed. You can make a comparison at your own convenience. It is not my intent to write a page-by-page critique of some of these books, but I have read enough of them to conclude that the authors lacked the proper perspective.

What I submit to you as a former president of the Jacksonville Youth Council NAACP, are eyewitness accounts, including my own. Trust me when I say we fought social injustice in Jacksonville as earnestly as those on the national level.

At age eleven, I joined the Jacksonville Youth Council National Association of Colored People (NAACP) at the invitation of Rutledge Henry Pearson, the Youth Council's Advisor and my eighth grade American History class instructor. At age 15, I would become president of the Youth Council NAACP. By the hundreds, young Blacks in Jacksonville responded to the call of Mr. Pearson to fight racism and segregation through this extraordinary organization.

The Jacksonville Youth Council NAACP represented non-violent, church going, committed, and dignified young people determined to be a part of the solution and not a part of the problem. They have held true to these values throughout their adult lives.

If segregation sought to remind Blacks of their perceived second-class citizenship in this country, then segregated lunch counters represented visible vestiges that served up daily insults. The time finally came when the Youth Council NAACP simply said, "enough is enough." Disregarding the personal physical peril, members of the Jacksonville Youth Council NAACP made the decision to confront Jacksonville's segregated policies and its accompanying Jim Crow laws.

Scores of Black heroes who participated in sit-in demonstrations surfaced across the United States. For the most part, those participants came from the campuses of Historical Black Colleges and Universities (HBCU). However, in Jacksonville, most of the demonstrators came from Black high schools. The peaceful protests of teenagers who dared to challenge segregated white lunch counters is not a myth or an urban legend. Nor is the attack by more than 200 whites with baseball bats and ax handles on 34 Black NAACP Youth Council members on August 27, 1960.

Today's generation must understand the circumstances and the times that led to this racially explosive and violent day in Jacksonville's history.

It is important to understand that because the philosophies of the Jacksonville Youth Council NAACP and Jacksonville's political and social establishment were so diametrically opposite, violence may have been inevitable. Yet, in a strange paradox, the violence perpetrated on the Jacksonville Youth Council NAACP that day changed the fight for civil rights in Jacksonville.

In an apparent effort to cover up the violence against the Jacksonville Youth Council NAACP and the sit-in demonstrations that preceded that momentous day, local print media and local television stations conveniently provided little or no news coverage. Local documentation about Ax Handle Saturday is conspicuously lacking. Virtually no photos of that horrific day exist. Thankfully, the Black media, even with obvious limitations, provided excellent news coverage.

Regardless of what you have heard or seen about sit-in demonstrations, it was never about eating a hot dog and drinking a Coke. It was always about human dignity and respect.

Blacks in Jacksonville endured an enormous amount of racism, discrimination, pain, and suffering in the fight for civil rights. They endeavored to leave a legacy and heritage from which we can benefit and of which we all can be proud.

It is my prayer that this book helps you appreciate the price they paid for freedom.

Table of Contents

Chapter 1

Jacksonville and the Duval County School System, circa late Fifties and early Sixties

"This fight for equality of educational opportunity is not an isolated struggle. All our struggles must tie in together and support one another . . . We must remain on the alert and push the struggle farther with all our might."

—Charles Hamilton Houston

At what age do you know enough about racism to recognize it? For many, the answer varies because the learning process actually begins at birth and continues through a series of ever-expanding experiences. When it is encountered as children, young Blacks may not be able to identify, classify, or understand it, but they know it just as sure as they know their names. I don't know when I understood racism; but when I first experienced it, I knew.

Traveling back and forth between Jacksonville, and Aiken, South Carolina, riding Greyhound Buses with my grandmother, I would learn quite a bit about racism in the fifties. I revisit those days many times in my mind. During those days, Jim Crow laws in the South required whites to sit in the front of the bus and Blacks to sit in the rear. Interestingly, my grandmother, who looked white, and I would sit together, anywhere we wanted, on the bus. Blacks riding on the bus would ask me if I worked for my grandmother because I did not have the physical traits to be riding with a white grandmother. After answering "no" for a while, I started saying "yes", because no one believed me when I said she was my grandmother.

On one occasion, my grandmother and I sat in the only available seats in the back of the bus. When seats emptied in the front after several white passengers disembarked at highway stops, the bus driver pulled to the side of the highway, and walked back to my grandmother to tell her that she could "move to a seat up front." After all, as a white woman, he certainly did not want her to sit in the back of the bus with the "coloreds." Boy did he ask for it. She told him her seat was fine. When he insisted she move, my grandmother adamantly remained in her seat, saying something respectful that meant to "mind your own business." The red-faced white bus driver returned to his driving.

My grandmother certainly qualified as a civil rights fighter in her own way. Dare I also call her a freedom rider? Given the times, and the circumstances, I now consider my grandmother a slight radical, though I did not think so at the time.

My mother, Janelle "Jan" Saunders Wilson, also defied the mores of segregation and Jim Crow Laws. She regularly held me so I could drink water out of a "WHITE" water fountain. She once asked a store manager about the "colored" water sign. "What color is it?" she asked. Maybe you would consider these actions small, but in retrospect, I consider them big.

I picked up interesting insights into racial attitudes from both my mother and my grandmother.

I spent most of my early formative years in church with my grandmother, Lizzie Foreman Williams. You never question attending church services when you spend time with your grandmother or your grandparents.

At West Friendship Missionary Baptist Church, the church schedule started with prayer meetings on Tuesdays, continued with Bible study on Wednesdays, and ended with Sunday school, Morning Worship, BYPU (Baptist Young People Union, which later became Baptist Training Union), and Evening Worship on Sundays. Add in Communion on the first Sunday, between morning worship and BYPU. My sister Joan and I regularly attended all services with our grandmother.

At age five, I entered first grade at West Jacksonville Elementary School, a segregated Black elementary school. During the days of segregation, Blacks always thought of their schools as community schools. Schools were a defined part of the community. Everyone knew everyone, and your parents knew your teachers—my mother certainly did. If you were brazen enough or stupid enough to get out of line or act up in class, you got a whipping at school from your teacher; then, when you got home, you got a whipping from your parents. Talking back to a parent ensured a fat lip. Unlike today, you did not consider getting a whipping as child abuse. It came with the territory. Getting out of line or acting up in class never made my things-to-do-or-consider-doing list.

At age six, I memorized the order of the 39 books in the Old Testament and the 27 books in the New Testament. Reverend Alvin Greene, my pastor at the West Friendship Missionary Baptist Church, asked me to memorize them, my grandmother wanted me to memorize them, so I memorized them.

Of course, after memorizing them, my grandmother would ask me to recite them for her and her friends. Grandmothers are like that. Granny picked the time and place. She always asked me to recite something. She would never ask me to say the books of the Bible, or tell me the names of the books of the Bible. I think the word "recite" just rang true for her. She would ask me to recite the books of the Bible for Mrs. Jennie McKinney or Mrs. Phoebe McCants or Mrs. Ruth Maultsby, who were some of my grandmother's closest friends. I would start at the beginning of the *Old Testament* with- *Genesis, Exodus, Leviticus, Numbers, Deuteronomy, Joshua, Judges, Ruth-* you get the picture. It did not make a difference when or to whom I would recite. When my grandmother wanted her favorite grandson to recite the books of the Bible, even for visitors, I recited them. By the way, I was also her only grandson. She called me a "dutiful grandson." You are a good child when you are "dutiful."

Into the *New Testament*, and a few minutes and 66 books later, I would end at *Revelations*. My grandmother was proud, my mother was proud, my sister was proud, my grandmother's friends were proud, and I was proud. Though she tried, Joan could not memorize the books of the Bible. She could not spell either.

In my second grade year at West Jacksonville, my grandmother and I relocated to Aiken, South Carolina. I enrolled in Aiken Graded School, a Black segregated elementary school. (Aiken County School District named the white elementary school Aiken Elementary School. Aiken County tore down Aiken Graded School

3

several years ago.) Although Joan and I visited Aiken with my grandmother many times, my sister remained in Jacksonville with my mother during this particular visit.

Mrs. Flossie Hammond taught my second grade class at Aiken Graded. If I had to pick from all the teachers that contributed to my educational experience, Mrs. Hammond would be near the top of my list.

Mrs. Flossie Hammond (and husband Thomas)
(Courtesy of the Gregg-Graniteville Library, University of South Carolina Aiken)

What sticks with me even to this day is that Mrs. Hammond taught me cursive writing—yes, cursive writing in the second grade!

At first, I could not get the hang of connecting the letters, and I thought I would never learn cursive writing. When she first asked me to write cursive words as a classroom assignment, I did not have a clue. I had never heard the word "cursive," let alone understanding what it meant. Quite naturally, Mrs. Hammond explained and demonstrated cursive writing. Anxious to complete what appeared to be an easy assignment, I proceeded to print several words, connecting each letter to the other with little squiggly lines. *There*, I said to myself, knowing I had accomplished this obviously easy assignment. Unfortunately, Mrs. Hammond crushed my newfound confidence when she said my little squiggly lines did not quite measure up. She continued to work with me until I understood. She took the time to make sure I did.

For me, Mrs. Hammond is one of those schoolteachers so beloved that, when I think of her, I just smile. Some of us have several Flossie Hammonds in our lives. She epitomized the caring and nurturing of a Black teacher who made a difference in your life—irrespective of the segregated circumstances. In my short enjoyable time in her class, she instilled in me a confidence that continued through my public school years (and to this day). Of course, my confidence also expanded through the encouragement and development of countless other Black schoolteachers, but Mrs. Hammond started it.

Based on a number of criteria, she would submit the necessary papers, evaluations, and recommendations that school year to have me "accelerated" or "skipped" to the third grade.

I left Jacksonville for Aiken in the second grade, and returned later that same school year in the third grade. Though my classmates changed, I continued to play with many of my second-grade friends every day during recess. By starting school at age five and being skipped a grade, my new classmates were two years older. It ushered in an interesting adjustment for me, and one that continued over the years.

Foreman was my grandmother's maiden name. Her married name was Williams. My grandmother's mother named her Lizzie, not Elizabeth, and it did not make a difference if you considered Lizzie short for Elizabeth. She would let you know it was Lizzie and not Elizabeth.

My grandmother's white father, Jim Foreman, took Lila Twiggs, my grandmother's pretty, fair-skinned Black mother, as his concubine or mistress—a common practice in the South. Only twelve when her mother died, my grandmother was the oldest of Jim Foreman's five Black children, and had the responsibility to raise her sisters and brothers. According to family members, Jim Foreman offered substantial parcels of land to my grandmother, and her sisters and brother, from his extensive holdings. She refused the offer, wanting no part of what some family members considered rightfully theirs, through birthright. My grandmother did not want anything from Jim Foreman. She and her sisters and brother would later move to Aiken.

Most historians in South Carolina consider the white Foreman family one of the founding families of the state of South Carolina. My grandmother, my grandaunts Ethel Foreman, Sadie Foreman, Beulah Foreman, and my granduncle Frank Foreman all had fair skin. They looked white. My grandmother had blue eyes. Whites in Aiken called my grandmother, my aunts, and my uncle "half-white." Blacks in Aiken considered them "high yellow". In Jacksonville, she was simply my grandmother.

Left, my grandmother, Lizzie Williams in her early twenties; top right, my granduncle Frank Foreman; middle right, my grandaunt, Sadie Foreman; and lower right, my grandaunts Beulah Perry and Ethel Johnson (photo courtesy Connie Foreman Daniels).

Many grandmothers of the time were members of a widow's club. In Jacksonville, my grandmother joined the Westside Widows' Club, which included Mrs. McKinney, Mrs. McCants, and Mrs. Maultsby. Joan and I were associate members (all grandchildren were associate members), and attended the meetings with her. They needed a secretary. My sister had trouble spelling, so my grandmother volunteered my services to take the minutes, and perform other necessary administrative support tasks. I worked pro-bono.

As we grew older and more mature, Joan and I sang at various locations throughout the west side of Jacksonville. Joan was quite a good singer. Homes of the Widows' Club members were our favorite venues, and "Bless This House" was our most requested song. We were such a popular act, we could have used an announcer and a booking agent. At our ages, it might have been a wee bit difficult negotiating with an agent—Joan was five, and I was seven.

By the way, over the years, my sister argues that by being two years younger, she did not know how to spell all the words required of a top-notch executive administrative assistant. I told her that excuse would not hold water, since even at age five, she should have known how to spell.

At age ten, I entered the seventh grade at James Weldon Johnson Junior High School in Jacksonville. It was 1954. In the main lobby of James Weldon Johnson Junior High School, hung a huge picture (at least it appeared huge to me) of James Weldon Johnson. Though I was only slightly familiar with Johnson, I knew he wrote what we considered the Negro National Anthem, "Lift Every Voice and Sing." I had no feel at the time for the greatness or the historical significance of James Weldon Johnson; I would soon learn, however.

After my family moved to Magnolia Gardens, Jacksonville's first Black subdivision, I transferred to Isaiah Blocker Junior High School. Our neighborhood boasted all the trappings of suburban America.

James Weldon Johnson Junior High School, a relatively new school, had the usual assortment of new and used equipment and furniture you expected in a segregated Black school. It had a gym with lockers, a separate cafeteria, and central heating and air-conditioning.

James Weldon Johnson Junior High School in 1956 (Courtesy Eartha White Collection, University of North Florida Library).

Isaiah Blocker Junior High School represented quite a change. Built as an elementary school in 1917, and originally named Davis Street Elementary School, Isaiah Blocker lacked a gym, lockers, shower facilities, and air conditioning. Radiator-type coils heated classrooms. It did, however, border an active railroad track, where passenger and freight trains ran often, and regularly.

Isaiah Blocker Junior High School. Note: picture is taken looking at the cafetorium, which was built in 1952. Isaiah Blocker was built in 1917. (Courtesy Eartha White Collection, University of North Florida Library).

On warm and hot days, classroom teachers kept Isaiah Blocker's cathedral-type windows open at the rear of the classroom, and opened transom windows at the front, hoping for cross-ventilation. It did not happen.

In the middle of a sandy athletic field near the railroad track stood a sandy, outdoor asphalt basketball court, which doubled as a "stand-up" classroom. Here, coaches taught dance and various physical education classes. When the wind blew, the court got sandier. When it rained or when the weather turned colder, we stayed in the "cafetorium." Our auditorium doubled and tripled as a classroom, study hall, and cafeteria. In fact, we often had our classes in the cafeteria-auditorium-classroom-study hall while others ate their lunch.

The Duval County School Board and the school superintendent declared that segregated Black schools were equal to white schools in Jacksonville, but they were not. Any walk through Jacksonville's segregated Black schools, followed by a walk through its segregated white schools, put the lie to that assertion. They could not camouflage how unequal they were, even when the occasional new Black school was built and opened.

Duval County's white schools received more resources, had larger budgets, spent more money, had newer and upgraded facilities, and always had sufficient materials and supplies.

The city's Black schools never had sufficient funding, never had adequate school and classroom supplies, and regularly received patronizing and condescending words from Duval County School System Board members, and the school superintendent about how they would look out for "the colored citizens, the colored students, and the colored schools." Of course, we even heard occasional references to "Nigra" schools.

In a believe-it-or-not scenario, some Black principals would actually return money at or near the end of the school year, to show the superintendent, and the School Board how well they managed their budgets. School officials, in turn, continued to pad the already full white school budgets, by reallocating the returned Black budget money to white schools to spend.

Duval County Schools had a Director of Negro Education, Dr. John Irving Elias Scott, who headed the Negro Education Division.

DIRECTORY OF NEGRO SCHOOLS

SCHOOL NAME AND NUMBER		ADDRESS
	NEGRO SCHOOLS OF DUVAL COUNTY	
	1955-56	
101	Negro Vocational School	521 West Ashley Street
1011	Adult Night School	
1017	Veterans Night School	
102	Oakland Elementary	1410 Tippin Street
104	Forest Park Elementary	Goodwin and Forest Streets
105	A. L. Lewis Elementary	600 Riverson Street
106	Long Branch Elementary	1230 East 27th Street
107	Douglas Anderson Elementary-Junior High	San Diego and White Street
108	College Park Elementary	1666 Pearce Street
116	Wesconnett Elementary-Junior High	Wesconnett, Florida
124	Moncrief Elementary	Route 3, Box 103
125	Arlington Elementary	Arlington, Florida
128	Susie E. Tolbert Elementary	1925 West 13th Street
133	Pickett Elementary	Pickett, Florida
135	Isaiah Blocker Junior High	2525 Davis Street
143	West Jacksonville Elementary	2071 Commonwealth Street
144	Jacksonville Beach Elementary	Jacksonville Beach, Florida
145	Darnell-Cookman Elementary	1901 Davis Street
146	Matthew W. Gilbert Junior-Senior High	1472 Franklin Street
148	Richard L. Brown Elementary	1535 Milnor Street
149	Smart Hope Livingston Elementary	Barber and Baldwin Streets
152	James Weldon Johnson Junior High	1840 West Ninth Street
153	New Stanton Senior High	1149 West 13th Street
154	John E. Ford Elementary	1057 West First Street
156	Baldwin Elementary-Junior High	Baldwin, Florida

BOARD MEMBERS

Ned P. Searcy   L. S. Sheffield*

V. T. Spivey   Martinez Baker

Lassiter Mason

TRUSTEES

Frank Sherman   Mrs. W. C. Pate

Spencer Ladd, Jr.

Mrs. Iva T. Sprinkle, Superintendent
C. E. Anderson, Director of Instruction
J. Irving E. Scott, Director of Negro Education
Mrs. Thelma H. Livingston, Supervisor, Guidance
Negro Schools

*Deceased

He had earned a Doctor of Philosophy Degree. During his tenure, Dr. Scott reported to two white-elected school superintendents: first to Iva T. Sprinkle, and later to Ish Brant, who did not come close to having Dr. Scott's professional educational credentials. Though eminently qualified, Dr. Scott disappointed many Blacks, who felt he did not fight hard enough to acquire more resources for Duval County's Black schools. Others simply wrote off his actions as those of a credentialed Black educator who went along to get along—a posture common among Blacks trying to survive the days of segregation. It generated distrust in the Black community—something that continues in the Black psyche today.

Looking back, you get the impression the Duval County School System wanted segregated Black schools to mark time educationally and not achieve even a reasonable modicum of educational success. The disgraceful lack of resources provided to Black schools and their teachers by the Duval County School System demonstrated a long-standing intentional policy of separate and unequal education. Nothing else can explain such meager resources for a public education during those crippling years of segregation.

On May 17, 1954, Chief Justice Earl Warren of the United States

Supreme Court delivered the historic, unanimous *Brown v. Board of Education of Topeka* decision:

"We come then to the question presented: Does segregation of children in public schools solely on the basis of race, even though the physical facilities and other 'tangible' factors may be equal, deprive the children of the minority group of equal educational opportunities? We believe that it does.

"We conclude that in the field of public education, the doctrine of 'separate but equal' has no place. Separate educational facilities are inherently unequal. Therefore, we hold that the plaintiffs and others similarly situated for whom the actions have been brought are, by reason of the segregation complained of, deprived of the equal protection of the laws guaranteed by the Fourteenth Amendment."

In a much-hailed decision, the highest court in this country declared, "Separate educational facilities are inherently unequal."

Nothing, however, changed in Jacksonville because of *Brown*. No attempts were made to implement the decision in the Duval County School System. Duval County continued its segregated schools and racist policies, and even hired a law firm to fight school integration with taxpayers' money. Duval County Schools would resist the decision, while continuing segregated business as usual.

School Board Plans To Fight Integration

However, the Duval County School Board appeared to have stepped up its construction of new schools as a way of stemming integration. From 1954-1957, three years after the Brown Decision, the Duval County School Board built 12 new schools.

Curiously, but not surprisingly, Duval County's School Board named several all white Jacksonville schools for Confederate Civil War Generals: e.g., Robert E. Lee, Kirby Smith, Jefferson Davis, Joseph Stilwell, and Jeb Stuart. Though insulting to the Black community, the political explanation was that these Civil War generals were Southern heroes fighting for their heritage and their way of life. In a further slap at the Black community, the School Board never considered the reality of slavery, and its violent viciousness, as counter arguments. In 1968, the Duval County School Board even named a high school after Nathan Bedford Forrest, the Confederate Civil War general who founded the Ku Klux Klan.

The KKK was founded on December 24, 1865 by six Confederate veterans in Pulaski, Tennessee. At its 1867 convention in Nashville, Tennessee, the KKK ordained its first Grand Wizard of the Invisible Empire—Nathan Bedford Forrest. Called the "Fort Pillow Butcher", Forrest claimed responsibility for massacring Negro troops who tried to surrender at Fort Pillow in April 1864. As one member of the Confederate 20th Tennessee Group reported, "The slaughter was awful." Forrest, pleased with the outcome, remarked, "The river was dyed with the blood of the slaughtered for 200 yards. It is hoped that these facts will demonstrate to the northern people that (N)egro soldiers cannot cope with Southerners." *Chicora Foundation*

After *Brown*, Blacks in Jacksonville continued to suffer the same indignities of school segregation. Every hand-me-down piece of furniture, secondhand equipment, and used textbook in Black schools had the name of the white school prominently etched, carved, or written in it. We did not like it, but we learned to make the necessary adjustments.

Most people today cannot begin to comprehend how Black schoolteachers taught Black students through an ever-enveloping veil of racism and discrimination. It was controlled segregated education in a controlled segregated school system. John Hurst Adams, a noted African Methodist Episcopal Bishop, opined that, if you control the education of a people, you control their minds.

Despite the obvious deficiencies in our segregated Black schools, we had a "community" of Black schoolteachers who cared, and manifested their caring in the classroom. They would not allow the system to control our minds. My list of heroic Black teachers is long, for many of them made the kinds of sacrifices well beyond being a professional educator. In addition to Mr. Pearson and Mrs. Hammond, I must acknowledge Mrs. Norma H. Bland (Speech, Drama, and English); Mr. Talbert Jackson (English and Journalism); Mrs. Camilla Thompson (Science); Mr. Adeline Cobb (English); Ms. Margaret Kinsey English (Algebra and Geometry); Ms. Caldonia Simpson (my first History teacher); Mr. Alvert Mackey (my first Algebra teacher); Miss Coatsie Jones (English); Richard T. Hadley (Music); Mrs. Thelma Argrett (my first homeroom teacher); Mrs. Vera Wiles (English); and Mrs. Emma Moran (Business). There were other equally dedicated Black teachers, but these prepared my classmates and me to meet the challenges of the world of tomorrow.

Dr. Martin Luther King Jr. once remarked that the hour between 11:00 a.m. and 12:00 noon on Sundays is the most segregated hour in this country. Nowhere did his comment vibrate louder than in Jacksonville, where Sundays saw little or no communication between white churches and Black churches in the fifties and sixties.

One of the interesting and little-known facts about the relations between white churches and Black churches in Jacksonville revolve around the joint history of Southern Baptist First Baptist Church, which is predominantly white, located in downtown Jacksonville, and Bethel Baptist Institutional Church, which is predominantly black and also located in downtown Jacksonville. First Baptist is the largest white Baptist church in Jacksonville and one of the largest in the country. Bethel Baptist Institutional Church was founded in 1838, is listed on the United States Registry of Historical Structures, and is the largest Black Baptist church in Jacksonville. Many in Jacksonville think Bethel Baptist Institutional Church grew out of First Baptist Church, when in fact, First Baptist grew out of Bethel. Though I will not expand upon it here, it is a fascinating history.

During the late fifties, several white ministers in Jacksonville would put their sermon texts in their church advertisements in local newspapers. In some of those texts, they justified segregation through Biblical scripture. Some would preach from the fourth chapter of *Genesis*, which deals with Cain being "cursed and marked" by God. The white minister interpreted the word "mark" to mean "black" skin color. They would use that part of scripture to explain God's curse against Blacks, and use it to rationalize segregation.

Jeremiah 13:23, a frequently cited scriptural passage, spoke of an Ethiopian changing his skin and a leopard changing its spots.

Then there is the Jacksonville minister who proclaimed that the Bible is the story of the Adamic race—God, he said, created a race of humans without souls who lived on the Earth before He created Adam, the first man. Various scholars have promoted this hypothesis at various times throughout history. Roman Emperor Julian the Apostate (circa 331–363 A.D.) and Calvinist theologian Isaac de La Peyrère (1596-1676) are two notable examples. Blacks do not have souls, they said, so God created Adam with a soul, and Adam became the first member of the white race.

Two of Jacksonville's white churches even allowed the Ku Klux Klan to hold fully robed rallies on their parking lots.

At the time, Jacksonville had a Mayor-City Commission-City Council form of government, and a separate County Commission. One would easily identify it as a politically expedient, yet rather cumbersome, good ol' boy system. Citizens voted citywide for Jacksonville's elected officials, or countywide for Duval County elected officials. There were district races, but candidates still ran at-large. Blacks could not run countywide or citywide at that time and win. I call it the good ol' boy system because Blacks represented 25% of registered voters in Jacksonville, but at-large elections diluted the Black vote and prevented the election of Blacks to public office.

Normal politics of the time had some Blacks collaborating with the white political establishment. These so-called Black political "bosses" represented themselves as necessary to make political contact in the Black community. Segregation being the consummate exploiter, at times they succeeded. Among other things, they printed a particular kind of campaign literature, which they called "tickets" which suggested for whom you should vote. These Negro wannabe power brokers created the impression that they could persuade the Black community to vote for certain white candidates if their names were on the tickets. White candidates had to pay them to get their names on the tickets, which were then supposedly distributed throughout the Black community. Sometimes, they included names of Black candidates to give the ticket a modicum of legitimacy. The ticket purported to represent various organizations, e.g. "The Citizens Committee for Better Government," "The Westside Good Government Council," and "The Negro Political Alliance," and whatever they called the organizational flavor of the month.

Most white candidates bought into the perceived reality that getting their names on these tickets helped them receive a significant percentage of African American votes.

Paying to get on one ticket did not get you on all tickets, although the same person might represent several tickets. White candidates paid to have their names listed on each ticket.

During those days, white candidates and the white political establishment in Jacksonville never spent real campaign dollars to solicit Black votes. They campaigned in the Black community on the cheap. Why spend money to campaign for Black votes, when lackeys in the Black community would do your bidding? Comparatively speaking, it would not cost much. Why care about the respect and the dignity of the Black vote? Just show up one Sunday morning at the church of one of the so-called representatives, receive an invitation to sit in the pulpit, and let the representative's pastor anoint you during the service.

White candidates, by relying on their newfound colored political friends, simply disrespected Black votes. Blacks, who did not give a damn about their community, were only concerned with lining their pockets at the expense of the Black community. Because there were no "Who gave it?" and "Who got it?" laws then, no one reported this ill-gotten income.

If a candidate won the election and the numbers included a sizable percentage of the Black vote, the so-called representatives claimed credit. If the candidate lost and his name appeared on just one ticket, he figured he did not pay enough. If a candidate won re-election, the colored "shysters" gladly claimed credit. Many Blacks were insulted when their votes were taken for granted especially since there was no proof these tickets helped a candidate get elected."

* * *

Then there was Ashley Street.

Carol Alexander, the director of the Ritz Theatre & Lavilla Museum has often said that LaVilla and the Ashley Street area was *the* "Harlem of the South."

Economic and social life in Jacksonville's Black community began with Ashley Street, the hub of the Black business district.

You had to visit Ashley Street in Jacksonville, much as you had to visit Beale Street in Memphis and Bourbon Street in New Orleans.

If you started at the corner of Broad Street and Ashley Street and walked west on either side of Ashley Street for three blocks, you would enjoy the essence of Black businesses and culture in Jacksonville. If you visited Ashley Street on any Sunday after church, you experienced an Easter Parade. You would see Black families, resplendent in their Sunday best, walking Ashley Street as they decided where they would eat Sunday dinner.

Those three blocks included high-quality, word-of-mouth-promoted culinary establishments such as Bubba Ford's Restaurant, Ivory's Chili Parlor, the Roosevelt Grill, the Busy Bee Restaurant, Singleton's Bar-B-Q, and the Boston Chop House.

If a man wanted to get a haircut or get his hair straightened, which was called "a process," he could choose from three stylish barbershops: the Artistic, the Roosevelt, and the Cosmopolitan.

If you wanted a soda at a soda fountain while you waited to get a prescription filled or if you wanted to shop while waiting, you could go to Reyno Pharmacy, Willie Smith Pharmacy, or the Imperial Drug Store.

If you wanted to shop for sartorial excellence, you would end up at Fashion's Men Shop, which featured premier head-to-toe menswear, including Botany 500 and Hart-Schaffner, and Marx suits, Stacy-Adams shoes, and Edmond Clapp shoes.

If a lady wanted her hair styled, she had her choice of at least five hair salons or beauty parlors.

If a lady or gentleman wanted shoes shined or repaired, or if a gentleman wanted his fedora cleaned and blocked, there was the Off Beat Shoe Shine Parlor.

You could stop and grab a quick hot dog at the Strand Hot Dog Stand.

You could order creamy fresh hot donuts at the Strand Donut Shop.

You could buy homemade candy at the Candy Kitchen.

To get your clothes cleaned, you had your choice of several dry-cleaning establishments.

If you wanted to go to a movie on Ashley Street, you headed to the Strand, Frolic, or the Roosevelt Theaters. Richard McKissick, the manager of all three theaters, could give you a run-down on all movies and upcoming features, and give you an update on who's who on Ashley Street.

You could also visit the Ritz Movie Theater three blocks away on Davis Street.

There were a number of taverns, bars, and clubs for your late afternoon and evening entertainment, all within that three-block walk along Ashley Street.

You could play the "Numbers," "Cuba," "Bolita," "Total," and the "Bond" on Ashley Street, at Red Dan's Smoke Shop. Bolita, the Numbers, and Cuba were illegal lottery gambling that originated in Harlem and spread throughout the South. You played the Bond throughout the week. On Saturdays, you played Bolita and Cuba through a surprisingly sophisticated structure of "bankers," house-men or house-women, and the "runners" who would take your bets—cash only—in the street, at your house, or at your business. Today's legal lottery games have many similarities to Bolita, Cuba, and Numbers.

Jacksonville was a major stop on the "Chitlin' Circuit," the colloquial name given a string of cities, usually in the South, with venues where Black celebrities would perform, usually for segregated Black audiences.

Jacksonville had become a regular Circuit venue because of its several major nightclubs, and especially the Two Spot Night Club. Owned by James "Charlie Ed" Craddock, who many referred to as Jacksonville's Cuba, Bolita, and Numbers king, The Two Spot was said to be the "...finest club in the country owned by a Negro". It got its name because of the large, bright, neon number 2 on the top of the building that housed the club. Most Blacks in Jacksonville considered the Two Spot, located in Duval County and a few yards from the Jacksonville City limit line, the crème de la crème. The hardwood dance floor could accommodate more than 1500 dancers. Equipped with modern conveniences and air conditioned throughout, a thousand persons could sit on the main floor and hundreds more in the balcony. Since segregation would not allow Black entertainers to stay at traditional hotels and motels, the Two Spot featured a number of hotel-styled and motel-styled rooms.

Preston Hale Craddock, Charlie Ed's son, added quite a few enticements to the Two Spot. You could dine in a restaurant that highlighted a one-of-a-kind glass-enclosed Bar-B-Q rotisserie. On its menu, in addition to excellent home cooked dining fare, the Two Spot restaurant featured a newly created culinary delight called curly-cues. For golfing pleasure, you could enjoy one of the few, if not the only, putt-putt golf courses for Blacks in the South. Of course, the Two Spot also had its own bar.

The Two Spot attracted such nationally noted Black performers as Billy Eckstine, Sarah Vaughn, Nat King Cole, Sam Cooke, Cab Calloway, Buddy Johnson, Lionel Hampton, James Brown and the Famous Flames, Jackie Wilson, Ruth Brown, and Fats Domino—the list is luxuriously long. Of course, the Two Spot was a segregated premier entertainment venue, which meant whites could attend, but could not mingle on the main dance floor with the Black crowd. When whites were admitted to the Two Spot, they were summarily ushered upstairs to sit in the balcony, segregated from the celebrity performers, and segregated from the exclusive Black audience. Under these circumstances, whites experienced a different kind of segregation, and certainly not the style to which they had grown accustomed.

Chapter 2

News for and about the Colored People of Jacksonville

"I am not concerned with your liking or disliking me.
All I ask is that you respect me as a human being."
—Jackie Robinson

How do you maintain your dignity in a segregated society designed to take your dignity? You continue to hold your head high.

You could have been the first Black Nobel Peace Prize winner from Jacksonville in the late Fifties and early Sixties, but news of this signal honor would have been relegated to a section of the *Florida Times-Union* called "News For and About the Colored People of Jacksonville."

STAR 4   · ·   THE FLORDA TIMES-UNION, JACKSO?

NEWS FOR AND ABOUT THE
COLORED PEOPLE
NEWS OFFICE PHONE EL 6-1601

News
For and About the
Colored People
Of Jacksonville
The Florida Times-Union
A Leader in the Growth and Development of Florida and the South for 95 Years

JACKSONVILLE, WEDNESDAY, MAY 11; 1960

Jacksonville had two daily newspapers in the late fifties and early sixties: the daily afternoon newspaper called the *Jacksonville Journal*; and the morning daily, the newspaper with the larger circulation, the *Florida Times-Union*.

Of the two daily editions of the *Florida Times-Union*, one edition had a black star at the top of the paper; the other edition did not. For home delivery, Black residences only received the "black star" edition of the *Florida Times-Union*, which included a section titled "News For and About the Colored People of Jacksonville." This section contained news about the Black community: church news, junior high school news, senior high school news, college news, social news, sports news, fraternity news, sorority news, wedding and engagement news, and obituaries.

White residences never received an edition with the black star. Because the *Florida Times Union* placed "News For and About the Colored People of Jacksonville" at the end of the newspaper, after the classified advertisement section, the paper added or eliminated the Black section for home delivery.

How did the *Florida Times Union* treat news about Florida Memorial College in St. Augustine, Florida (now Florida Memorial University and located in Miami, Florida), Bethune-Cookman College (now Bethune Cookman University) in Daytona Beach, Florida Agricultural and Mechanical University (FAMU) in Tallahassee, Florida, and Edward Waters College? Not surprisingly, they also relegated news about these significant institutions of higher education to the pages of "News For and About the Colored People of Jacksonville".

These great Historical Black Colleges and Universities (HBCUs), representing veritable treasure troves of noteworthy information, somehow did not warrant any news coverage in the main body of the newspaper.

Were these great Historical Black Colleges and Universities significant to Blacks? You bet they were! Yet, Florida Memorial College, Bethune Cookman College, Florida A & M University and Edward Waters College somehow, did not warrant any news coverage in the main body of the newspaper.

On the other hand, Black papers like the *Amsterdam News*, the national edition of the *Pittsburgh Courier*, the Florida edition of the *Pittsburgh Courier*, and national Black magazines like *Jet* and *Ebony* were invaluable during this period.

Local Black newspapers like the *Florida Star*, published by Eric O. Simpson, represented one of the few news sources for the Black community during the civil rights movement. In fact, the Black press achieved much-deserved national recognition because they were the only media fairly and consistently covering the civil rights movement.

For a brief time during my high school years, I delivered *Florida*

Times-Union newspapers in the Magnolia Gardens subdivision where I lived. Occasionally, Black paper routes in areas outside the city limits had white customers. I did not have any white customers. I operated my regular newspaper route either on bicycle or on foot. On the other hand, delivering newspapers on routes with white customers usually required a car because of the route size and its location. Black newspapermen delivered these routes with one prime service directive—do not deliver the black-star edition of the *Florida Times-Union* to the home of a white customer. Consequences for failure were tremendous. Some Black newspapermen actually lost their jobs because they inadvertently delivered a black-star edition *Florida Times-Union* newspaper to the home of a white customer.

There were also circumstances when the *Florida Times Union* did not print a black star newspaper edition for home delivery. Our Black newspaper route supervisor told us the newspaper had a "short print run."

It actually meant we would not have a black-star newspaper to deliver to our Black customers, who complained bitterly. However, their complaints did not cause anyone to lose their job.

Whites did not want to read about Blacks in their daily newspaper, and the *Florida Times Union* apparently accommodated them. Conversely, Blacks never saw themselves objectively included in the *Times-Union* newspaper, which some would say is akin to American history devoid of relevant contributions by Blacks.

During this period of segregated life in Jacksonville, the newspaper's regular sports section almost never recognized the accomplishments of Black high school athletes. Like regular news, sports news about Blacks in Jacksonville only made its way to the "News For and About the Colored People" section. With the segregation of sports news, whites only read about the exploits of whites on the athletic field. Segregation did not afford them the opportunity to know any of physically gifted and outstanding Black high school athletes growing up in the Jacksonville community.

And there were plenty. Jacksonville's talented Black high school athletes in the fifties read like a "Who's Who" in Black sports. They include: Bob Hayes, Alfred Austin, Herbert Blackshear, Tommy Chandler, Mathis "Plute" Daniel, Alfred Denson, Nathaniel Graddick,

Malcolm Graham, Willie Bussey, Jake Hagins, Arlexie Gray, Robert Haywood, Willie Haywood, Claude Hill, James "Gator" Johnson, Oliver Joyce, Robert Lucas, Curtis Miranda, Henry Nash, Julian "Bill" Walton, Bernell Sumpter, Charles "Knots" Sutton, Charles "Tree Top" Thompson, and Billy "Bowlegs" Walker. These are just a few of the consensus great Black high school athletes whom I saw play during my junior high and high school years. Most of the white sports community in Jacksonville and the white community of Jacksonville probably never heard of most of these names, and certainly were unaware of them during their high school years. Yet many of their sports exploits were legendary.

In a parallel to Negro education, in the State of Florida, a Negro High School Sports Division referred to as the Florida Interscholastic Athletic Association, dealt only with Negro sports.

White sports reporters, for instance, covering high school athletics, wrote feature stories about Robert E. Lee High School track athlete David Mann, and his 1958-59 City of Jacksonville high school 100-yard dash track and field record of 9.9 seconds. However, during Black high school track meets, Robert Lee "Crow" Hayes (Crow was Bob Hayes's nickname in high school), who attended Matthew William Gilbert High School, Alfred Austin of New Stanton High School, and Malcolm Graham of Northwestern Junior-Senior High School, regularly bested Mann's times.

At one Jacksonville Black high school track meet in 1958 at Wilder Park, Hayes won the 100-yard dash with a time of 9.6; Austin placed second at 9.7; and Graham third at 9.8. Hayes and Austin battled each other regularly in track meets during high school and consistently ran the 100-yard dash under 10 seconds.

In the Black community, we knew of Bob Hayes's football heroics at Matthew W. Gilbert High School. We knew that he lettered in four sports. And we knew that Bob was first and foremost a football player, who happened to be fast—real fast.

When Bob played baseball at Gilbert, Dr. Alvin G. White, who coached Matthew Gilbert's baseball team, employed a unique defense using Bob in the outfield. He would position the left fielder near the left field line, the right fielder near the right field line, and let Bob

Hayes patrol an expanded left-right-centerfield. Bob could literally run down everything hit to the outfield. He was that fast.

Bob Hayes, born in Jacksonville on December 20, 1942, graduated from Matthew William Gilbert High School on the east side of Jacksonville and attended Florida Agricultural and Mechanical University (FAMU) on a football scholarship. During his college days at FAMU, Bob established his supremacy as a track star without peer when he set the 100-yard dash mark of 9.1 seconds in 1962, a mere two years after high school. At collegiate track meets, Hayes blew everyone away.

At several Historically Black College and University track meets—segregated of course—Bob ran such incredible times that track meet coordinators and official timers would round off Bob's official winning time to the next tenth of a second. They knew no one would believe that a Black track athlete could run the times that their stopwatches and other official timing devices were showing. If we consider the segregated culture and climate in the South then, they were probably right.

In the 1964 Summer Olympics in Tokyo, Japan, Bob's track legend took on mythic proportions. He won the 100-meter dash "going away," which is virtually unheard of in an Olympics event with international talent. However, his 400-meter relay anchor leg, a few days later, is the stuff of which we make legends. It was such an over the top individual effort, you stand in tribute, and certainly in awe, even watching the replay.

Hayes received the relay baton in sixth place as the anchor for the United States 400-meter relay team. Bud Palmer and Jim Simpson, the NBC network announcers doing the commentary, had already conceded the United States, who lost this event in the 1960 Olympics, would probably lose again.

Then Bob Hayes ran what most sports observers consider the greatest anchor leg in the history of the Summer Olympics and in the history of the 400-meter relay. His anchor leg time of less than nine seconds is so fast and so unheard of that Olympic officials timing the event with various timing devices all acknowledged they probably made an error. Noted sports columnist Ralph Wiley put his time at 8.6! The Los Angeles Times called it "the most astonishing sprint of all time." No one runs an anchor leg for a 400-meter relay in eight and six-tenth seconds—no one, that is, but Bob Hayes.

Bob Hayes

Hayes entered two events in the 1964 Tokyo Olympic Games, and won two Olympic gold medals. Usually you crown the track athlete who wins the 100-meter dash in the Summer Olympics "the world's fastest human" because of the world-class international competition. Bob deserved that title for winning the 100-meter dash, but he could have just as easily earned it for his 400-meter relay anchor leg.

Of course, as Richard Pryor would say, we all knew the boy had "po-tain-chul" (potential for the uninitiated). At least, we knew it in Jacksonville's Black community because we saw it regularly. Bob epitomized competitiveness and athleticism. Nevertheless, segregation kept all of Jacksonville's white community from seeing Bob, because racism prevailed also on the athletic field.

Bob Hayes would later have an outstanding career in the NFL with the Dallas Cowboys. When he made his debut with the Dallas Cowboys in 1965, his Olympic sprinter's speed forced teams to change how they played defense. His speed literally changed pass defenses in the National Football League from man to man coverage to zone coverage. In his rookie season with the Cowboys, Hayes had 1,000 yards and 12 touchdowns while leading the NFL with an astonishing average (at that time) of 21.8 yards a catch. He still holds or held numerous pass receiving and punt return records in the NFL. He is the only athlete in the history of sport to win an Olympic gold medal and a Super Bowl Champions' ring (with the Cowboys). Hayes died prematurely in 2002 due to failing health. It is truly unforgivable that Robert "Bullet Bob" Hayes is not a member of the National Football League Hall of Fame.

Back in our days of segregated Jacksonville, we also knew Alfred Austin, one of the premier football halfbacks in the state. Alfred graduated from New Stanton High school in 1959 and attended Florida A&M University on a track scholarship. He had the kind of blazing speed that allowed him to turn the corner and outrun everyone to the end zone. Like Bob Hayes, Al represented another in a tremendously long string of talented Black athletes that Jacksonville reduced in importance by limiting both coverage and exposure to the "News For and About the Colored People of Jacksonville."

For two years as high school athletic competitors, Al Austin and Bob Hayes battled each other at Jacksonville's segregated Black high school track meets, recording great 100-yard dash times and 440-yard relay anchor legs. Then they joined as track teammates at FAMU.

Florida A&M's 440-yard dash relay team ran the fastest college time in the nation in 1961 and 1962, with Austin and Hayes both recording blistering times. Named the Outstanding Performer in 1962 at the Drake Relays, Bob Hayes and relay teammates Alfred Austin, Robert Harris, and Robert Paremore posted a national record—40.8 seconds in the 440-yard dash relay. Austin calls them the three Roberts and an Al. He also was a conference champion javelin thrower and is a member of Florida A&M's athletic Hall of Fame.

After graduating from Florida A&M University, Austin joined the Duval County School System as a schoolteacher. Principal Alvin G. White initially hired Austin as the track coach at Jean Ribault High School. He would later assign Austin as the Ribault Girls' basketball team coach after the existing girls' basketball team coach quit. Austin coached girls' basketball at Ribault High School for 26 years.

Austin's Jean Ribault high school girls' basketball teams won an astounding eight State of Florida Girls' Basketball Championships, which is a State of Florida high school record. His record at Ribault was 632-55. His teams won 21 district, 19 conference, 17 regional and 12 sectional titles. Austin is a member of the Florida Coaches' Hall of Fame and was also named USA Today Newspaper Girl's Basketball Coach of the Year in 2002. Many revere him today as both a high school girls' basketball coach, and as an athletic director in Jacksonville's high schools.

Alfred Austin easily could have coached football or other sports at Ribault and would have been as successful. He is that talented and that good. However, the white community never knew of this tremendous talent through his high school and college years. Al continues as the Athletic Director at Jean Ribault High School after retiring from coaching.

As Black athletes, Bob Hayes and Alfred Austin were the quintessence of superior Jacksonville high school athletes. Despite shackled with undeserved chains of segregation and racism, they represented the City of Jacksonville well.

Chapter 3

Rutledge Pearson and the Jacksonville Youth Council NAACP

"Those who have no record of what their forebears have accomplished lose the inspiration, which comes from the teaching of biography and history."
—Carter G. Woodson

He had sandy red hair, stood about six feet two inches tall, was fair-skinned, and had a magnetic presence as he walked the halls of Isaiah Blocker. A stranger visiting Isaiah Blocker Junior High School, probably would have considered Rutledge Pearson, the dean, or president of the school, based on the respect he commanded.

Rutledge Henry Pearson (courtesy of Mary Ann Pearson).

I transferred from James Weldon Johnson Junior High School to Isaiah Blocker Junior High School in 1955. The public schools of Jacksonville, in 1955, mirrored the segregated South: separate textbooks, separate and unequal equipment, and separate and unequal facilities.

Only a few new things filtered down to us at Isaiah Blocker. We were just part of the overall Duval County Schools Educational System, Negro Division—still separate and very much unequal.

As a new student at Isaiah Blocker, I did not know many students or teachers. As I talked with several students during my transfer-student honeymoon period, one of the students asked my favorite subject. I said American History. They suggested I ask to be assigned to Mr. Pearson's American History class.

I later overheard some of the same students remark how difficult Mr. Pearson's classes were. Did I smell a set-up for a new transfer student? As an A-B Honor Roll student who loved history, I figured I could handle this challenge, so I asked for and got the assignment to Mr. Pearson's class. It is obvious to me now that my transfer to Isaiah Blocker Junior High School and subsequent meeting of Mr. Pearson were parts of God's plan.

My first day in Mr. Pearson's class is vivid to me even today. He had a particular routine for his classes during the first week of a school year. He asked members of the class to walk me, the new student, through the routine, because I had transferred to his class during the middle of the first semester. The lines went as follows:

"The textbook for our American History class is *Life in These United States*. It is on the Duval County School Board's list of approved textbooks. The McMillan Publishing Company publishes it. The authors are Robert Johnson and Martin Richards. Published in 1953, it has 352 pages. LEAVE IT HOME!"

Mr. Pearson did not teach American History from the slanted views of authors of textbooks approved by a segregated school system. He did use the book and its table of contents as a guide to follow the course syllabus and the school system's requirements. At the end of the school year, Mr. Pearson's American History textbooks had the least wear of any textbooks in the school.

Also during my first day in his class, Mr. Pearson asked me to give some historical background on James Weldon Johnson. Of course, I had just transferred from James Weldon Johnson, and should have some knowledge about this great Black man.

I started by saying that James Weldon Johnson had written "Lift Every Voice and Sing." I knew nothing about his being the first principal of Stanton High School, or of his being the first executive secretary of the NAACP. I did not know or say he was born in Jacksonville. In short, I could not say very much about him. While doing my best impression of being cool, I stammered and stuttered, trying to find something to say, and I lost a perfect opportunity to describe the historical relevance of this great man. I quickly began to wonder if I could transfer to an easier American History class. Now, for the first time, despite my self-proclaimed love for American History, someone had to help me out in a history class. I promised myself it would be the last time. And I did not transfer to another class.

Mr. Pearson's American History classroom work and assignments demanded information-gathering, and research that you would have expected of a *high school* American History class. He wanted us to seriously study Negro History (the vernacular at the time). Remember, this was a *junior* high school American History class.

Mr. Pearson gave us this definition of history: "History is a narration of facts . . . arranged in chronological order . . . with their cause and effect." He wanted to make sure, and wanted us to make sure, that the narrated facts were actually facts. He also wanted us, as Dr. Cornel West would say, to refuse to settle for mediocrity.

We worked in small groups or in "history classroom research teams." We studied Toussaint L'Ouverture, Benjamin Banneker, Dr. Daniel Hale Williams, Dr. Charles Drew, Matt Henson, Chrispus Attucks, etc. We identified contemporary Blacks all over this country, and wrote letters to them: such people as Jackie Robinson, Althea Gibson, and John Hope Franklin, and to members of the NAACP Legal Defense Fund Team who had won the *Brown* decision—Thurgood Marshall, James Nabrit, Spottswood Robinson, Constance Baker Motley, George E. C. Hayes and Robert Carter.

When a team received a response, a member would read it aloud in class. We had to type classroom projects and assignments, double-space them as you would for a college term paper, and include reference pages. Computers did not exist then. We submitted all completed work in folders or binders.

George E. C. Hayes, Thurgood Marshall, and James Nabrit on the steps of the United States Supreme Court after the Brown Decision (courtesy of the NAACP).

We were required to take notes during panel discussions, and ask questions of our classmate presenters. Every class member had to ask at least one question. Mr. Pearson would test the class on the subject and the contents of the panel discussion the following day. His classroom lectures required full participation, and he gave us written exams. Again, remember, this is a *junior* high school American History class.

Dr. Carter G. Woodson founded Negro History Week, and quickly became one of our favorite persons. In 1926, Woodson initiated the annual February observance of Negro History Week. He chose February because February 12 was Abraham Lincoln's birthday, and because February 14 was the accepted birthday of Frederick Douglass. There are other arguably valid reasons for his using February. The Thirteenth Amendment to the Constitution was signed into law in January 1863, but official word about abolishing slavery did not reach most slaves until February 1863. (Word did not reach slaves in Texas until June 19, thus the Juneteenth holiday observances in Texas.) Woodson hoped Negro History Week would compensate somewhat for the unfair treatment he felt Blacks received in American history.

Most public school American History textbooks during the fifties included only a few references to Blacks: Booker T. Washington and George Washington Carver or Frederick Douglass's writings. Though important to the history of this country, they certainly are not the only Blacks who made salient contributions to America. In Mr. Pearson's class, we did not have to look forward to just a week or month of Negro History—we had Negro History every day. When Mr. Pearson's classes displayed their exhibits during Negro History Week, they easily rivaled high school exhibits.

Studying American history without also explaining the contributions of Blacks yields an undesirable consequence: If you have no clue about the historical contributions made to this country by my ancestors, you have a lack of respect for me as a Black person. As a Black man, I have an obligation to learn about those historical contributions, so I can explain them to you. I also have an obligation to show you documented proof that Blacks helped to found and settle this country.

Mr. Pearson not only taught us in his American History and Civics classes, but he encouraged us to join an organization called the Youth Council of the National Association for the Advancement of Colored People. At that time, he served as one of two advisors to the Jacksonville Youth Council NAACP.

I knew about the NAACP, but frankly had no clue about the NAACP Youth Council, though it did sound quite interesting. Mr. Pearson used a particular saying when he talked with us about the NAACP and the struggle for human dignity and respect. He simply said, "Freedom is not free," which resonated with me.

Mr. Pearson also encouraged Black schoolteachers at Isaiah Blocker to join the NAACP, and sought support for the NAACP from the community. Getting Blacks in Jacksonville to join the NAACP became one of his priorities.

Not all Black teachers were eager to join the NAACP. Some were afraid, and felt joining the organization would jeopardize their jobs. Others didn't recognize the need to join the NAACP. However, many Black schoolteachers did join, like Ms. Gertrude Glover, who also taught at Isaiah Blocker. Not only did Ms. Glover join the NAACP, she gave Mr. Pearson her check for a $500 NAACP Life Membership.

From left, Rutledge Pearson, Dr. Alvin Gross, Ms. Gertrude Glover, Roy Wilkins (Courtesy of Mary Ann Pearson).

It was the largest check I can remember seeing at the time. Making the sacrifice and paying that kind of money for a Life NAACP Membership dramatized Mr. Pearson's saying that "freedom was not free."

Mr. Pearson marshaled financial support for the NAACP from the Black professional community. A member of Alpha Phi Alpha Fraternity, he would make frequent presentations and membership appeals to Black professional and civic groups, fraternities, and sororities.

Most Black doctors and dentists in Jacksonville financially supported the NAACP—like Dr. Jean C. Downing, Dr. Hunter Satterwhite, Dr. James Henderson, Dr. O. W. McIntosh, Dr. L. B. Childs, Dr. L. G. Childs, Dr. E. Washington, and Dr. W. W. Schell.

Some white businesses in the Black community also financially supported NAACP, and some white businessmen even joined the NAACP. Marvin Ganson, who owned the Kozy Korner convenience stores; Arv Rothschild, the General Manager of the Strand and Roosevelt Theaters, and the Moncrief and Skyview Drive-in Theaters; and Dr. Alvin Gross, an optometrist, are whites who immediately come to mind.

Mr. Pearson's classroom teaching, and his involvement with the NAACP outside the classroom, took a lot of courage in the fifties. He and his family even moved into the predominantly white Springfield neighborhood, which we considered one of *the* racist neighborhoods in Jacksonville at that time. At the ripe "old" age of eleven, I could not understand or appreciate the width and breadth of Mr. Pearson's courage, but I would become a quick learner.

In essence, here was:

A Black schoolteacher in Jacksonville who ignored and refused to use the approved Duval County School System American History textbook that excluded many relevant contributions by Blacks;

A Black schoolteacher in Jacksonville who taught outside of the public education box by extolling the contributions of Blacks in American History;

A Black schoolteacher in Jacksonville who encouraged both students and schoolteachers to join the NAACP while actively marshalling the resources of the Black community;

A Black schoolteacher in Jacksonville instrumental in getting whites to actively support and join the NAACP;

A Black schoolteacher who proved, even in Jacksonville, that the color of your skin should not be a prerequisite for, or a condition to, the purchase of a home in any neighborhood in Jacksonville, Florida.

As I said, Mr. Pearson personified courage.

Harry T. Moore, a Black schoolteacher whose life we studied in Mr. Pearson's class, is one of the great and courageous unsung heroes of the civil rights movement. You will not read a lot about Harry T. Moore. You will not see his name mentioned in talks about the civil rights movement. Yet, Harry T. Moore and his wife Harriette Moore were the first civil rights martyrs.

I can see parallels between Harry T. Moore and Mr. Pearson. Both fought for human dignity and respect inside and outside the classroom. It took a great deal of courage to face continuing and overwhelming opposition.

Harry T. Moore, born in Houston, Florida, near Live Oak on November 18, 1905, briefly lived in Jacksonville with relatives. In 1934, Moore moved to Brevard County, Florida, and established the Brevard County Branch of the NAACP.

Harry T. Moore (Courtesy the Florida Photographic Collection).

Moore led the campaign for equal pay for Black schoolteachers in Florida's schools and founded the Florida Progressive Voters League, which succeeded in tripling the enrollment of registered Black voters. It also brought him derision and scorn in many quarters.

Moore and his wife Harriette were both schoolteachers, and both were fired from their teaching jobs because of Moore's activism. He would become a full-time, paid staffer for the Florida NAACP, and achieved great success for it. By the end of 1948, the NAACP had over 10,000 members in Florida.

In 1949, Harry Moore campaigned against the wrongful conviction of three Blacks for the alleged rape of a white woman in Groveland, Florida. Because of his efforts and the efforts of NAACP attorney Thurgood Marshall, the United States Supreme Court in 1951 ordered a new trial. Before the new trial, Willis McCall, the infamous sheriff of Lake County, shot two of the Black defendants while in his custody—"mysterious circumstances" were cited. McCall killed one of the men, and seriously wounded the other. Moore's call for McCall's suspension took tremendous courage considering the absolute community control by Southern law enforcement officers. A month later, on December 25, 1951, a bomb exploded under Moore's house, killing him and his wife.

The deaths of Harry T. Moore and Harriette Moore rocked the nation, resulting in dozens of rallies around the country. President Truman and Florida Governor Fuller Warren were flooded with telegrams and protest letters. News of Moore's murder triggered a national and international outcry. Protestors even registered complaints at the United Nations. President Truman sent the FBI to investigate. The State of Florida, where eleven other race-related bombings had occurred earlier that year, found itself the focus of outrage and scorn for its treatment of Blacks. Although the FBI and other law enforcement agencies said they suspected members of the Ku Klux Klan, no arrests were made in the Moores' deaths.

To this day, Harry T. Moore and his wife Harriette are the only husband and wife to give their lives to the movement. Certainly, Harry Moore's life became a testament that freedom is not free. He paid the ultimate price for his commitment to our freedom.

Rutledge Henry Pearson, born September 6, 1929, was the youngest son of Mr. and Mrs. Lloyd H. Pearson Sr. A 1947 graduate of New Stanton Senior High School, Mr. Pearson attended Huston-Tillotson College (now University) in Austin, Texas, on a baseball scholarship. He would meet his wife, Mary Ann Johnson of Waco, Texas, while attending Huston-Tillotson.

The Pearson Family. Top row left, Mary Ann Pearson, Samuel O. Pearson, Rutledge H. Pearson, Lloyd N. Pearson Jr., Frank Pearson, Delores Pearson. 2ⁿᵈ row-Delores Z. Pearson, Mildred Pearson (Lloyd Junior's wife), Mary Crumley (holding Rutledge Jr.) Lloyd N. Pearson, Sr., (holding Frank Crumley), Ruth Pearson, Barbara Pearson, Myrtle Pearson, (Frank's wife). 3ʳᵈ row (seated) Gregory Pearson, Antoinette "Bitsey" Gatlin, Patricia Pearson, Brenda Pearson, Mildred "Lucy" Pearson, Wynetta Pearson (picture courtesy of Mary Ann Pearson.

In addition to his sports prowess, Mr. Pearson, an outstanding student leader and a devout Christian, served as a member of the renowned Houston-Tillotson College Quartet, the student director of the Houston-Tillotson College Choir, and president of his graduating class. He received his Bachelor of Arts in Sociology from Huston-Tillotson in 1951.

According to Mary Ann Pearson, Medgar Evers, a revered icon in civil rights history, was their classmate and friend at Huston-Tillotson College.

After losing contact for a number of years after college, Mr. Pearson and Medgar Evers rekindled their friendship when each led the civil rights struggle in their respective states: Medgar Evers in Mississippi, and Mr. Pearson in Florida.

In 1963, at Mr. Pearson's invitation, Mr. Evers spoke at an NAACP function in Jacksonville. Mr. Pearson would have returned the favor later that year by speaking at a similar NAACP function in Mississippi.

However, before he could keep that speaking engagement, Byron de la Beckwith would assassinate Medgar Evers at his home in Jackson, Mississippi. It would take law enforcement officials more than 30 years to bring Byron de la Beckwith to justice.

An outstanding baseball player, Mr. Pearson played professional baseball for the Birmingham Black Barons of the Negro League, and with the inimitable "Goose" Tatum, then with the Indianapolis Clowns professional baseball team, and a future Harlem Globetrotter. Pearson would have played professional baseball in the Major Leagues for the Jacksonville Beach Sea Birds of the Milwaukee Braves farm system, but Jacksonville Beach baseball park officials closed the park to keep him from playing. This act changed his life, and put him on a path to dedicate his life to the struggle for human dignity and respect.

Medgar Evers (Courtesy the NAACP papers).

Rodney L. Hurst Sr.

Arguably the best high school baseball coach in Jacksonville, Mr. Pearson coached some of the finest high school baseball players in New Stanton High School and Jacksonville history. Many of them would go on to play college ball: Mathis "Plute" Daniel at Allen University; Robert Lucas, Roy T. Thomas, Nathan Graddick, Maurice Williams, and Larry Pauline at Florida A & M University; Telfair Shields, Henry Nash, and James "Gator" Johnson at Allen University; and Alphonso Stanfield, who attended Langston University in Oklahoma.

Chapter 4

Earl Johnson

"Not to know is bad; not to wish to know is worse."
—African proverb

He had a voice that sounded as if it rumbled from the depths of a cave. With his deep, rich baritone, he could have been on the bill of the Metropolitan Opera or narrating an important classical work. Earl M. Johnson was neither opera star nor actor, but as the local attorney of record for the NAACP, he would magnificently represent the NAACP and the Youth Council many times.

Johnson was the legal thread that sewed through Jacksonville throughout the late fifties and the sixties. He is another in a long list of revered civil rights heroes from the Jacksonville community. He was the NAACP Chief Counsel in Jacksonville. His law partner was Leander Shaw, also Legal Counsel for the NAACP, who would later become the first Black Chief Justice of the Florida State Supreme Court.

Because so many of us depended upon Earl Johnson and Leander Shaw for legal support and advice, we would have kept their telephone numbers on speed dial, if we had such a feature then. Few knew about the countless meetings and strategy sessions they both held collectively and Johnson held individually in person and telephonically with Thurgood Marshall, Constance Baker Motley, Robert Carter, Mrs. Ruby Hurley, Roy Wilkins, Bob Saunders, and other NAACP officials throughout this country. Johnson and Shaw met weekly, if not daily, with us, Mr. Pearson, and other local NAACP officials in Jacksonville. At the time, the nature of the movement required it.

The NAACP has one basic philosophy. This is an oversimplification, but the organization works to put itself out of business. If it wins the ongoing fight against racial discrimination, racism, sexism, and other forms of discrimination, we would not need the NAACP.

Unfortunately, the NAACP probably works as hard now as it ever did. Since its founding in 1909, the NAACP remains in the forefront of the struggle for human dignity and respect.

Thurgood Marshall founded the NAACP Legal Defense and Educational Fund, Inc. (LDF) in 1940. Although LDF's primary purpose is to provide legal assistance to poor Blacks, its work over the years has brought justice to all Americans. Since 1957, the Legal Defense Fund has been an entirely separate organization from the National Association for the Advancement of Colored People (NAACP). It has a national office in New York, and regional offices in Washington, D.C. and Los Angeles. Hundreds of cooperating attorneys throughout the country, including Earl Johnson and Leander Shaw, assisted two dozen LDF staff lawyers.

In 1960, Johnson filed the NAACP school desegregation suit against the Duval County School System on behalf of Sadie Braxton and her children, Sharon and Daly Braxton.

Like Mr. Pearson, Johnson and Shaw lived with constant death threats and vicious telephone calls. Though many of us wrote off the lunatic fringe during those days, we painfully know now that you never take such threats or telephone calls lightly.

Chapter 5

The Black Church

"My main point here is that if you are the child of God, then God is a part of you. In your imagination, God is supposed to look like you. And when you accept a picture of the deity assigned to you by another people, you become the spiritual prisoners of that other people."
—John Henrik Clarke

The civil rights movement in Jacksonville would not have survived without the support of Black pastors and their churches. Though many Black pastors welcomed us to their churches, other Black pastors did not. Considering their perceived status in the community, then and now, it was rather surprising who they were.

We received solid and unequivocal support from the Right Reverend Sherman L. Green, then Bishop of the Eleventh Episcopal District of the African Methodist Episcopal (AME) Church, which included the State of Florida, and the Bahamas. Not one AME minister or AME church turned us down when we wanted to use their church for an NAACP Youth Council meeting, an NAACP Adult Branch meeting, or an NAACP Mass Meeting. AME ministers, such as Reverend J. S. Johnson of St. Stephens AME Church, Reverend R. J. Blaine of St. Paul AME Church, Reverend J. T. McMillan of Grant Memorial AME Church, and Mt. Zion AME Church, were all staunch supporters of the NAACP.

We could also depend upon Reverend Robert H. Wilson, and historic Bethel Baptist Institutional Church to host a number of important NAACP mass meetings, which included a major address by Reverend A. Leon Lowery, State NAACP President from Tampa, Florida. We could depend on Reverend Wilbert Miller and the Laura Street Presbyterian Church, where Mr. Pearson and his family worshipped, and where we

41

planned strategy for the sit-ins; Reverend Charles Dailey and the First Baptist Church of Oakland; Reverend Richard L. Wilson, my grandmother's minister and my minister until age 11, and the West Friendship Missionary Baptist Church; Reverend A. J. Hughes and St. John's Baptist Church; Reverend D. B. Barnes and the Sweetfield Baptist Church; Reverend B. L. Wynn and Abyssinia Baptist; and Reverend John B. F. Franklin and Ebenezer Methodist Church. These churches were not only major supporters of the NAACP, but they provided some of our essential support during our key phase of the civil rights era.

During the fifties and sixties, the Black Church represented our spiritual strength, our sanctuary, our refuge, our informational news network, and the major meeting location for NAACP meetings. We did not have large auditoriums and other venues where we could meet during these days of segregation.

Those Black ministers who were advocates of civil rights gave the movement a lot of its spiritual direction and spiritual energy by leading through example.

Reverend J. S. Johnson (courtesy Eartha White Collection, University of North Florida Library).

Reverend J. S. Johnson, the pastor of St. Stephen's A.M.E. Church, was a fire-and-brimstone minister, yet a venerable fatherly figure. He dearly loved the civil rights movement.

When Reverend Johnson addressed the Youth Council or an NAACP Mass Meeting, he would often invoke the saying, "The die is cast . . . and war is declared on the enemies of freedom everywhere." He spoke with such conviction, fervor, and enthusiasm that it felt like the very foundation of the church would shake. Plutarch attributes those words—"the die is cast"—to Julius Caesar when Caesar crossed the River Rubicon. He meant that Caesar had crossed the river, and there was no going back. However, when Reverend Johnson spoke those words and adapted them to his style, they seemed tailor-made for the struggle.

Black ministers, who were proponents of the movement, always knew what to say and when to say it. For those of us in the Youth Council, it made a difference. Their words lit the fire that we did our best to keep burning.

Regrettably, several churches were antagonistic to the NAACP during that time. Such behavior added clarity to Mr. Pearson's statement, "Freedom is not free." You have to pay a price and make sacrifices for freedom. We felt that Black ministers should certainly understand and identify with that truth. But some Black churches appeared to have serious ties to Jacksonville's white political establishment, and dared not encourage or support the movement. Other Black churches simply could not ignore the legitimacy of the organization and offered begrudging support to the NAACP. Still other Black churches appeared overly fearful of harmful consequences and renounced any support of the NAACP.

Jackie Robinson came to Jacksonville in February 1957 to speak to an NAACP mass meeting kicking off the Jacksonville's NAACP Annual Life Membership drive. We wanted him to speak at a location that would allow a substantial number of people to hear his message. Shiloh Metropolitan Baptist Church had the largest seating capacity of any Black church in Jacksonville, and that became the unanimous venue choice of the NAACP.

Rodney L. Hurst Sr.

Baseball Great Jackie Robinson (Courtesy the NAACP Papers).

We asked Reverend A. B. Coleman Sr., the pastor of Shiloh, if the NAACP could hold the meeting at Shiloh with Jackie Robinson as the speaker. He said we could, but that he would have to charge the NAACP $100 for using the church. We could not believe that any church, let alone a prominent Black church like Shiloh, would charge the NAACP a $100 fee, or any fee, to hold a meeting featuring baseball great and civil rights pioneer Jackie Robinson. Most churches would have gladly offered their church sanctuary without a charge. After all, it *was* Jackie Robinson!

Despite the amount of money the local NAACP chapter received through its memberships, $100 represented a significant amount of money then. Asking for donations to help underwrite many of the expenses associated with the organization's civil rights activities went on non-stop. Nothing we said to Reverend Coleman dissuaded him from charging the NAACP $100.

That night, Jackie Robinson spoke to an overflow crowd, and the NAACP paid Shiloh the $100. We never had another mass meeting in Shiloh during the late fifties or early sixties.

Another prominent Black Baptist church in Jacksonville, Mt. Ararat Baptist Church, never held an NAACP meeting, not an NAACP Mass Meeting or an NAACP Youth Council meeting, during the late fifties and early sixties.

One day during a Youth Council meeting, we discussed where we would hold some of our upcoming Youth Council meetings—we held them throughout the community. Someone asked why we had not yet met at Mt. Ararat Baptist Church. I responded, "Because they don't want us there."

"When was the last time you asked the pastor if we could hold a meeting there?" a Youth Council member asked. Mr. Pearson and the Youth Council agreed that approaching the pastor of Mt. Ararat again would be fair. We agreed to contact the church's minister, Reverend Dallas Graham, to see if we could hold a Youth Council meeting and possibly a mass meeting at Mt. Ararat Baptist Church.

After making an appointment, Mr. Pearson and I went to the church and met with Reverend Graham. He told us he did not have a problem with our meeting at the church, but the chairman of Mt. Ararat's trustee board, Frank Hampton, kept the church's calendar at his business, which was located across the street. We would have to clear availability dates with him. We walked across the street to meet Mr. Hampton at his business, a Gulf Oil Service Station. We explained to Mr. Hampton that Reverend Graham referred us to him to get a possible date either to hold an NAACP mass meeting or a Youth Council meeting at Mt. Ararat Baptist Church. Without so much as looking at the church's calendar and barely acknowledging Mr. Pearson and me, Mr. Hampton told us somewhat contentiously that the Church did not have any available meeting dates for the next three months.

Despite Hampton's belligerent attitude, Mr. Pearson made one last pitch, asking if we could get a date after the three months. Frank told us we would have to come back after three months to check the church's availability.

We thanked him for his time, and left, certain that Mt. Ararat Baptist Church did not regard the NAACP warmly.

Ironically, Mr. Hampton and Rev. Graham had been involved in the civil rights movement prior to the sixties. In fact, Mr. Hampton brought Dr. King to Jacksonville to speak at Mt. Ararat on behalf of his local civil rights group, the Duval County Citizens Benefit Committee.

After that, Hampton's group and the NAACP did not associate with one another, nor did Frank Hampton and his local civil rights group have a continuing relationship with Dr. King. For whatever reason best known by its members and the church leadership, Mt. Ararat never granted permission to the NAACP or the NAACP Youth Council to convene in its edifice during this important phase of the Civil Rights Movement in Jacksonville.

Chapter 6

The Jacksonville Youth Council NAACP and the 1960 Sit-in Demonstrations

"Salvation for a race, nation or class must come from within. Freedom is never granted; it is won. Justice is never given; it is exacted; and the struggle must be continuous for freedom is never a final fact, but a continuing evolving process to higher and higher levels of human, social, economic, political, and religious relationships."
—A. Philip Randolph

Mrs. Pearson never knew from one day to the next when we would show up at her house to ride with Mr. Pearson to Wednesday Youth Council meetings. Nor did she know when we'd put our feet under her dinner table, whether she fixed enough food or not.

I attended my first Jacksonville Youth Council NAACP meeting in November 1955 at the historic Masonic Temple Building at 410 Broad Street.

The Masonic Temple

The Black Masonic Temple in Jacksonville became the focal point for many of Jacksonville's Black community commercial and fraternal activities. Today it is the headquarters of the Masons of the State of Florida Grand East. Built under the leadership of Grand Master Jon H. Dickerson in 1912, the Masonic Temple featured elements of the commercial style of Louis H. Sullivan, and occupied the third through the sixth floors. Anderson Bank, the first bank for Blacks in Jacksonville, occupied the basement level.

Teenagers as well as young adults attended the Youth Council meeting. My mother gave me permission to stay after school so I could attend the meeting. I would usually ride the school bus to and from Isaiah Blocker. I told my mother, "Mr. Pearson will bring me home after the meeting," as he did for many Youth Council members. In fact, his 1956 green Pontiac and later his 1958 green and white Pontiac station wagon would travel countless miles throughout Jacksonville, throughout the South, and up the Eastern coastline for the NAACP and the Youth Council NAACP.

Though chartered by the NAACP National Youth Office as a Youth Council, the Jacksonville Youth Council really functioned as a Youth Council/Young Adult Council. NAACP Youth Council ages started at 13 and continued to 18 under the NAACP's national office structure. Nevertheless, we expanded the ages—with the office's blessing. We continued as the Jacksonville, Florida Youth Council NAACP.

Youth Council meetings started at 7:30 p.m on Wednesday nights. Sylvia Tyson, a Naval WAVE stationed at the Jacksonville Naval Air Station, served as the president of the Youth Council.

Robert Butts, the first Black and the first person from Jacksonville to join the Peace Corps, served as first vice president, and Leroy Bass as the second vice president. When Butts left for the Peace Corps, Barbara Simmons (Van Blake) replaced him and would later become Youth Council President.

There were two Youth Council NAACP adult advisors at that time. Mr. Emmanuel Eaves, a local businessman with major family roots in Jacksonville, served briefly with Mr. Pearson as Youth Council advisor.

Youth Council NAACP meetings formally followed an agenda that adhered to *Robert's Rules of Order*. One permanent agenda item included updating members on current civil rights events, and all current events, generally. At various points during the meetings, both Mr. Eaves and Mr. Pearson would discuss issues at the national level and explain the NAACP's position on them. We certainly discussed the *Brown v. Board of Education of Topeka* Supreme Court decision. The issue of school integration was always timely, and never left our agenda.

After Mr. Eaves left, Mr. Pearson became the sole advisor to the Youth Council. I was eleven when I first joined, and just sitting at the meetings, listening to Youth Council plans, and getting regular updates on civil rights activities became a formative experience.

I met Constance Baker Motley and Thurgood Marshall the following year when they both visited Jacksonville to meet with NAACP officials and to address NAACP mass meetings. First, you just stare, then you come to your senses—and you keep staring. To the nation, and to us, they were superstars.

The late United States Supreme Court Justice Thurgood Marshall (Courtesy the NAACP papers).

I brought my $1.00 with me to pay the Youth Council membership fee. I might have been prone to spend the money on something else. I had a little part-time job, so my one dollar represented hard-earned money. I joined the Youth Council NAACP that night. Having a membership in a real organization filled me with great pride. Joining the NAACP

Youth Council became my initial step up to the "freedom is not free" plate. From that time onward, I remained in a continual "freedom is not free" learning curve.

Youth Council meetings mirrored Mr. Pearson's American History class: informative, interesting, topical, and stimulating. As boring as they might seem to others, I looked forward to Wednesday night Youth Council meetings, which I permanently affixed on my social and civic meetings calendar.

We would sing "freedom songs" as a special part of all Youth Council meetings. It got us pumped. Singing those songs somehow gave me a new appreciation for what they represented. The songs and spirituals included: "I'm Gonna' Sit at the Council Table"; "Freedom"; "I've Been 'Buked and I've Been Scorned"; "I Got Shoes"; "We Shall Overcome," the movement's anthem; and one of the greatest hymns written, and my favorite, "Lift Every Voice and Sing, then referred to as the Negro National Anthem.

Confronting racism and the segregated southern way of life in the fifties and the sixties turned out to be a necessary experience for Blacks who realized "freedom is not free."

With African Americans continually facing an unrelenting barrage of increased violence, lack of respect, and racist hatred, Mr. Pearson understood the need to arm us at least with the legacy of our proud Black ancestry.

Since we could not pick up any approved public school system textbooks and read about positive contributions and accomplishments of Blacks, our Black teachers used those deliberate omissions as opportunities to teach us about our rich heritage.

During Youth Council meetings, Mr. Pearson occasionally allowed those of us who were not Youth Council Officers to preside over the meetings. Youth Council Officers and members would analyze our ability to chair a meeting as well as our knowledge of *Robert's Rules of Order*. Not only did we become acclimated to officiating during meetings, but we also developed exceptional public speaking skills.

On our way home after Youth Council meetings, Mr. Pearson's Pontiac became a venue for a mobile seminar on public speaking. "Never lock your knees," he would say. "Be comfortable at the podium and relax." "You know what you want to say—say it." "You don't have time to be nervous." I would remember.

He also taught me how to outline and write speeches. In eighth grade, I wrote speeches. The following year, I ran for president of the Isaiah Blocker Junior High School Ninth Grade Class and won.

After Barbara Simmons (Van Blake) left the Youth Council to attend Howard University, the Youth Council elected me president in 1959. Also elected were Alton Yates, first vice president; Marjorie Meeks, Youth Council secretary; and Henry Gardner, Youth Council Treasurer. Henry attended New Stanton High School. Marjorie and I were seniors at Northwestern Junior-Senior High School. We were quite a team. We worked well together because we never looked at the scorecard to see who got the credit.

We moved our Youth Council Wednesday night meetings to the Laura Street Presbyterian Church Youth Center on Laura Street between State and Union. We called Laura Street the Pearson Church. It is the church where Mr. Pearson and his immediate family and all of the Pearson family attended services, with Reverend Wilbert Miller as pastor.

The Jacksonville Youth Council NAACP, with Mr. Rutledge Pearson as the advisor, organized the sit-in demonstrations in Jacksonville without the assistance, or collaboration, of other organizations. Our Youth Council membership consisted of junior high and high school students from Jacksonville, college students from Edward Waters College, college students from Jacksonville who were home for the summer, and young adults who were out of school.

There were other organizations. SNCC is a great organization and certainly paid its dues during the movement, but SNCC did not organize or contribute to the sit-in demonstrations in Jacksonville in 1960. There were absolutely no SNCC "organizers" in Jacksonville. Most in the movement considered Jacksonville an "NAACP town" because of its long-standing relationship to the NAACP.

Several author's and historians have written or implied that SNCC helped to organize the Jacksonville sit-in demonstrations. They concentrated on gathering data from those we will call revisionists did not take into account that critical details may very well have been altered or modified. Despite the consequences of mediocre investigation and inferior research, they proceeded with erroneous information.

This book should eliminate any unrealistic, imaginary, and fabricated storytelling with regard to SNCC's participation or presence and set the record straight.

I vividly recall what we dealt with in Mr. Pearson's American History class and how we viewed many history book authors and historians. Thanks to Mr. Pearson, I realize that the "narration of facts" should at least be that—factual.

Jacksonville Hemming Park (Courtesy Florida Photographic Collection).

Confederate Monument Hemming Park (now known as Hemming Plaza) is a park in the center of downtown Jacksonville. Cohen Brothers, J. C. Penney's, F. W. Woolworth, and various shoe and specialty stores all opened into Hemming Plaza at that time.

Charles C. Hemming, a native of St. Augustine who spent his early life in Jacksonville and served as a private in the Jacksonville Light Infantry during the Civil War, donated the monument to the City of Jacksonville. In appreciation of his gift, the city of Jacksonville on October 26, 1899, named the park after him. At the top of the monument is the figure of a Confederate soldier in winter uniform, standing at ease with his musket resting on the ground. On his cap are the initials, "J.L.I.", representing the Jacksonville Light Infantry.

Hemming Park represented a fascinating study of people movement in Jacksonville. Laura Street, the eastern boundary of Hemming Park, was a major public bus transportation hub in the fifties and sixties. Every morning, hundreds of Blacks waited there to catch buses coming from the south side of Jacksonville—buses filled primarily with white riders who worked in the downtown area. After white passengers disembarked from buses on Laura Street, Black passengers would board, traveling to some of these same areas where the white passengers had come, including white homes where many Blacks worked.

We often discussed how whites did not mind Blacks working in their homes, keeping their children and cooking their meals, but did not want Blacks sitting next to them at a lunch counter or a restaurant. Such a seeming contradiction made for many lively discussions in Youth Council meetings.

In 1960, Woolworth represented one of the many vestiges of segregation that openly insulted Blacks daily. As a retail store that opened its doors to the public, Woolworth, as well as W. T. Grant, Kress, McCrorys, and Cohen Brothers, would accept your money as a shopper at one counter, but not accept your money or allow you to shop at another.

Hemming Park looking to the west. Note Woolworth to the left as a part of the J.C. Penney Building. The Robert Meyer Hotel is at the rear. In the middle of the park is the Confederate Soldier Statue. (Courtesy Florida Photographic Collection)

Located at the corner of Monroe and Hogan in downtown Jacksonville, Woolworth Department Store was one of several major downtown stores. In today's terms, Woolworth was an anchor store downtown. You would have also considered J. C. Penney an anchor store. Both stores were located next to each other in the J. C. Penney Building and shared a common wall. You could literally walk from J. C. Penney to F. W. Woolworth without going outside, and behind both stores stood the Robert Meyer Hotel. Together, the three structures occupied an entire city block. (The recently built Charles E. Bennett Federal Court House now sits on that site).

When you entered Woolworth from Hogan Street and looked to the left, you could see a lunch counter spanning the entire Monroe Street side of the store. Eighty-four lunch counter seats were punctuated by spacious customer-serving bays and bright windows.

You could stop and eat at Woolworth's convenient lunch counter after spending time shopping in Woolworth or after shopping downtown. You could, that is, if you were white. For Blacks, an invisible sign read, "Lunch Counter, FOR WHITES ONLY."

If Black shoppers wanted to eat in Woolworth after shopping, the process worked differently. Woolworth wanted you to spend your money, but only where they wanted you to spend your money.

Enter Woolworth again. The white lunch counter is on your left. If you started walking to the rear of the store, you would walk past the cosmetics counter;

then walk past the costume jewelry counter;

then walk past the popcorn popper;

then walk past the candy counter;

then walk past the women's clothes counter;

then walk past the men's clothes counter;

then walk past the children clothes counter;

then walk past the "White" and "Colored" water fountains;

then walk past the work shoes counter;

then walk past the dress shoes counter;

then walk past the bedroom shoes counter;

then walk past the picture frames and mirrors counter;

then walk past the aquarium supplies counter;

then walk past the stairs leading upstairs to restrooms marked "White Women," "White Men," "Colored Women," "Colored Men";

then walk past the pet food and pet supplies counter;

then walk past the house plants;

then walk past the gardening supplies counter;

AND THEN, and only then, would you see the Colored lunch counter, with its fifteen seats and no windows.

You could eat at the Colored lunch counter or you could walk to the restaurants and other eating establishments on Ashley Street, about six or seven blocks away. You also had a third option; you could wait until you got home. *Bottom line*: Woolworth accepted money from Black shoppers at one counter and rejected their money at another.

When we started sit-in demonstrations, we wanted everyone to know eating a hot dog and drinking a Coke would not be our focus. Human dignity and respect would be our fundamental focus, along with making segregation extremely expensive. Woolworth, Grant, Kress, McCrory, and other department stores all catered to daily lunch crowds with menus that featured fresh hot foods. In the age before microwaves, you could not refrigerate and quickly reheat anything.

We knew, based on information from the NAACP National Youth Office and from NAACP college chapters, that most stores would close their white lunch counters whenever Black students sat down there. You cannot serve grilled cheese sandwiches, hot dogs, BLT sandwiches, garden vegetables for salads and sandwiches, and hot foods prepared for a daily crowd if your lunch counter is closed. You could not store the food overnight and serve it the next day. Who wanted reheated hot dogs or bacon that you had to put in the oven again? You had to throw the food out. We wanted store owners and their managers to know that maintaining their segregated and discriminatory policies would be expensive.

However, confronting a store about segregated white lunch counters would only be part of our strategy. Challenging the lunch counters and the designation of colored and white racial categories meant challenging the system and a way of life.

We understood sit-ins could turn ugly and violent. Even at our ages, while not dwelling on it, we did not naively underestimate the danger. Mr. Pearson obviously understood the danger it posed, as well as his responsibility to ensure that both parents and students

Rodney L. Hurst Sr.

understood the risks. We did not appreciate the burden placed on Mr. Pearson as our adult advisor.

The Greensboro Four- Jibreel Khazan (formerly Ezell Blair), Franklin Eugene McCain, Joseph Alfred McNeil, and David Richmond sitting at a white lunch counter in Woolworth in Greensboro, North Carolina, February 1960.

When the wave of sit-in demonstrations began February 1, 1960, with Jibreel Khazan (formerly Ezell Blair), Franklin Eugene McCain, Joseph Alfred McNeil, and David Richmond sitting at a "for whites only" lunch counter at a Woolworth's in downtown Greensboro, North Carolina, no one could have imagined the aftermath.

Notwithstanding the Montgomery Bus Boycott, the legacy of Mrs. Rosa Parks, Dr. Martin Luther King Jr., this courageous act by four young Black students from North Carolina A&T University changed the direction of the civil rights movement.

This first sit-down demonstration motivated students at Historically Black College and University campuses throughout the country. In the days that followed, demonstrators in more than 100 cities picketed segregated stores and participated in sit-in demonstrations. Most demonstrators were Black students, although some white students joined the demonstrations. Many thought it important that sit-in demonstrators look dignified and dress in their Sunday best. It became signally important to project an image of dignity.

In some cities, stores closed their lunch counters when students sat-in. In other cities, law enforcement officials arrested demonstrators for trespassing. In some of those cities where arrests took place, inmates beat demonstrators in jail, or law enforcement officials beat them under the guise of resisting arrest and a myriad of other charges. Law enforcement officials stood by, in a number of documented cases, and allowed inmates to rape Black female high school and college students. Of course, the press reported few of these cases.

By comparison today, you would consider Blacks sitting at a segregated white lunch counter as tame stuff. But in the fifties and the sixties, Blacks sitting at a segregated white lunch counter was deemed a violent confrontation to the racial comfort system in the South. For white Americans, as a friend would say, "It was something that was so not going to happen." After all, there were appropriately stationed lunch counters expressly for Negroes.

We employed the philosophy of "passive resistance" and non-violence during our sit-in demonstrations. If provoked, we would not fight back. Of course, we would defend ourselves if attacked, but non-violence became the prevailing approach to sit-ins. Not many would or could embrace that philosophy but we felt it necessary to confront the racist elements of American culture. It is the same strategy and philosophy used by Mahatma Gandhi when he fought and died for India's freedom from British colonialism; and the same philosophy of Dr. Martin Luther King Jr. as he fought and died for freedom and justice in the United States of America.

After completing our research, we decided our first sit-in would take place on Saturday, August 13, 1960, at Woolworth Department Store. Though we focused on Woolworth because of its strategic location, we also targeted the restaurant in Cohen Brothers (which now houses Jacksonville's City Hall) and the lunch counters at W. T. Grant Department store, Kress Department store, and McCrory Department store.

Some Youth Council members had trouble sleeping on the Friday before August 13, 1960. Most of us experienced some anxiety leading up to that first sit-in demonstration. However, it did not linger with an advisor like Mr. Pearson.

On the morning of August 13, 1960, we had more than 100 Youth Council members ready to go. In our Youth Council meeting that Saturday morning, we prayed and sang our freedom songs. Leaving Laura Street Presbyterian Church Youth Center on foot en route to Woolworth in groups of twos and threes alerted no one.

We arrived at Woolworth a little after 11:00 a.m., well aware of what we were preparing to do. I called that morning the "beginning of a mission." Understanding that "freedom is not free," we had to step up to the plate; we had to stand up and be counted; we had to let everyone know what we were made of—all the clichés applied. We were not attending an after-school dance or a sock hop. Our mission was simple and serious.

Youth Council members-From left, George Tutson, Jacqueline Stephens, Colbert Britt, Joan Holzendorf, Helen Britt, and Rodney Hurst standing in front of the NAACP Office. (Courtesy the Pittsburgh Courier)

Upon entering Woolworth, we planned to purchase an item to demonstrate that the store would accept our money. No problem there. However, if, Woolworth refused to serve us at the white lunch counter, we would use the earlier purchase to show the contradiction in Woolworth's store policy—they would accept our money at one counter, while summarily refusing it at another.

Each of us always made sure we had enough money in our pocket just in case they decided to serve us at the counter. We would later joke with each other about newspaper headlines that read, "Youth Council members arrested, not for sitting in, but for not having money to pay for the food they ordered."

Each demonstration had sit-in captains, and only the captains would talk to the media. We did not want conflicting "official" comments. Alton Yates and I were captains of the first sit-in on August 13, 1960.

After purchasing our items, and at an agreed upon signal, Youth Council NAACP members followed me, Alton, and Marjorie Meeks to the white lunch counter. Jacksonville's sit-in era had begun.

After sitting down, a white waitress announced loudly to all who could hear that "coloreds are not served at this lunch counter. This is the white lunch counter. The colored lunch counter is at the back of the store." We did not move or say anything. White waitresses working behind the lunch counters began to huddle while giving us that "you don't belong here" stare.

A little later, James Word, the manager of Woolworth, came and read a prepared statement that in effect said Woolworth reserves the right to refuse to serve anyone. He also gave us directions to the colored lunch counter. We still did not move. I told Mr. Word that we were here for service. He would later tell several of us that he was experiencing his first sit-in demonstration. I often wondered if he knew we were too. He gave the order to close the lunch counter.

We continued to sit. Just in case Woolworth store officials decided to re-open the lunch counter, we had agreed to sit through the entire lunch period. A crowd of white onlookers began to assemble and show displeasure by shouting tasty morsels of racial epithets. They obviously blamed us for Woolworth's decision to close the lunch counter.

After several sit-ins, we developed a friendship of sorts with Woolworth manager James Word. He would recognize us when we returned. He would tell the late George Tutson, a Youth Council member, and a student at Morris Brown College, that if left to him, he would have integrated the lunch counters in a split second. However, managing a store in the South obligated him and Woolworth to follow the dictates of segregation laws and policies.

In this first sit-in, both the white and Black press interviewed us. In fact, this is one of the only pictures (page 60) of that first sit-in on August 13, 1960, showing the press interviewing Alton Yates (left) and me (right). Eric Simpson, the publisher of the *Florida Star*, is standing behind us.

Racial slurs continued to flow from the hostile crowd.

We were not surprised—we had prepared for most of the possible extracurricular happenings, such as being stuck with pins and other sharp objects, unnoticed kicks to our lower legs, and being pushed by the assembled white crowd of males and females as we left the lunch counter. One woman blocked my path and stepped on my foot, heel first. It did not matter. I kept walking out of the store, trying not to turn toward the crowd or acknowledge the immediate pain. A woman's shoe heel makes an impression on the toe of your shoe, and on your foot.

Jacksonville's first sit-in demonstration, August 13, 1960. Reporters talk with Alton Yates, first-vice president and Rodney Hurst, president of the Jacksonville Youth Council NAACP (Courtesy Rodney L. Hurst, Sr.).

It was never about a hot dog and a Coke!

Other members of the Youth Council during that first demonstration including Marjorie Meeks, left, and Mary Alice King. (Picture courtesy Rodney L. Hurst, Sr.)

During a demonstration at Woolworth, Youth Council member and sit-in demonstrator Roderick Freeman on right. Note the man with the walking cane, who whittled the tip of the cane with a knife until the cane had a sharp point; then he walked (with assistance) behind each demonstrator sticking them in their back with the cane. (Picture courtesy Rodney L. Hurst, Sr.)

More pictures of the first demonstration at Woolworth Department Store, August 13, 1960

Though we left the lunch counter separately, we all had similar rough encounters with the white crowd.

It did not take us long to walk back to Laura Street Presbyterian Church Youth Center, though we occasionally looked over our shoulders to see if anyone was following.

I anxiously looked through my Sunday black-star edition of the *Florida Times-Union* to see how the press would cover this first sit-in.

Nothing about the sit-ins made the front-page—not a shock, at least to me. Surely, they would not carry the story in "News for about the Colored People of Jacksonville." They did not. In fact, the *Times-Union* did not report anything about the sit-in anywhere in the paper. Although sit-in demonstrations were significant news, lack of local coverage was an indication of what we could expect.

It was never about a hot dog and a Coke!

News Black-out On Jax Sit-Ins Shows Danger In Press Monopoly

Jacksonville's colored citizens got just a little taste of what life could be like in a communist state where the news is censored and the people are provided with only such information as the dictators desire them to have.

More than two weeks ago a group of young men and women began picketing a South Myrtle Ave and Forest Ave. super-market in protest of the firm's employment policy which hired only one Negro in the face of the fact that, according to the youths, more than seventy-five parent of the firm's patronage come from colored citizens. But not a word was mentioned in the daily papers.

On Saturday Aug. 13 another group of Negro youths composed of members of the NAACP Youth Council began a series of lunch counter sit-in demonstrations which, as the days went by were carried to Woolworth's, Kress and Cohens. Still not a word of these protests was printed in either of the fast moving daily newspapers, at least one of which has a large number of Negro subscribers who get for their money a segregated version of the news favorable to Negroes.

In this news-hungry day and age even the most untutored person knows that news is those events that interest and or affect people. The sit-in demonstrations have been treated as news—big news—in virtually every section of the country wherever they have occurred, for the simple reason that the purpose for which they were designed has a significant bearing upon civilization and our social and economic structure.

It was pointed out by Negro leaders that knowing the segregated policies of the dailies they were hardly expected to support the ideas of the sit-in demonstrations. But they have found that they were somewhat naive in believing that as newspapers dedicated to disseminating the news in the community, the local dailies would have reported the news of such vital events to all occurring in our community.

The fact that the news black-out of the demonstrations was lifted only after the move to curb them and the arrest of Negro demonstrators were made has swerved to awaken many to the ...tening underlying situation that really exists.

One Jaxon said: "It means that a mob could machine-gun down a group of colored citizens and not a word would be reported in the daily press if forces didn't want it known."

The observer went on to say the situation that exists in Jacksonville whereby the main news sources are controlled by one force is bad for the colored people as well as the white.... It means that public opinion could be formulated and dominated by one source.....Under such a monopolized press we could find ourselves so utterly brainwashed that we will be voting for measures that would deny us of our rights and priviledges.

The speaker went on to say that this news black-out not only emphasizes the need for the Negro press but also how foolish it is for colored citizens to support a daily paper that maintains a policy toward Negroes such as we have in Jacksonville. He urged that Jaxons takes steps to provide its citizens with a daily Negro newspaper, or at least a twice weekly one to start with.

(Editorial in the Florida Star, by Editor/Publisher, Eric O. Simpson.)

Chapter 7

Richard Charles Parker

"A fully functional multiracial society cannot be achieved without a sense of history and open, honest dialogue."

—Dr. Cornel West

Richard Charles Parker came to the Laura Street Presbyterian Church Youth Center one summer day in 1960 and asked to participate in the Jacksonville Youth Council lunch counter demonstrations. He had read about the demonstrations in a Tallahassee newspaper, he said, and wanted to aid the cause. Richard Charles Parker, a college student at Florida State University, happened to be the first white person who asked to join the sit-in demonstrations in Jacksonville.

Richard Charles Parker (Courtesy of Rodney L. Hurst Sr.).

Though sit-in demonstrations raised the consciousness of the nation about the evils of racism and discrimination, National NAACP headquarters cautioned NAACP youth councils and college chapters about would-be demonstrators about whom we knew very little. F.B.I. Director J. Edgar Hoover certainly wanted to tag the NAACP as subversive, Communist, or worse. For those reasons, we were leery of Parker at first. We were all mindful and fearful that someone could come to undermine the sit-ins.

Many whites and the national press in this country felt that direct-action activities such as sit-in demonstrations would undermine the country, and labeled them as Communist-inspired or subversive, or both. Racists already had a clear view of the NAACP. With that backdrop, the NAACP used tremendous caution to ensure no one joined the organization or participated in direct action demonstrations without some preliminary checking. After talking with Parker and doing what we considered a diligent background check, we were convinced he was not a Communist and legitimately wanted to participate in the sit-ins.

Richard Charles Parker was 25 years of age, a native of Massachusetts, and a junior at Florida State University. On his very first day sitting in at the Woolworth lunch counter, whites and the media assumed he was the leader of the sit-ins. The crowd of onlookers showered him with the standard "nigger-lover" and "race-mixer" names.

Most observers always thought if whites were involved they were the leaders of a civil rights demonstration in the South.

Construction workers building the Florida National Bank Building south of Woolworth, between Monroe Street and Adams Street, regularly ate at Woolworth. They emphatically voiced their anger against us for disrupting their lunch schedules when Woolworth chose to close the lunch counter.

Woolworth employed several strategies to continue to feed their regular lunch bunch. They tried to serve their lunch customers at one designated bay. Customers would stand behind each other, and as one person would finish eating, another person would sit. That worked for a while, until several white Navy wives, sympathetic to the sit-ins and sensing what was happening, sat one day at the bay counter and ordered extra sodas to share with us "sit-inners," who were sitting close to them. We appreciated the offer, but did not drink the sodas. When Woolworth's strategy to keep part of the segregated lunch counter open fell apart, they once again closed the entire lunch counter.

Woolworth later resorted to changing its lunch hours to begin 30 minutes to 45 minutes earlier to foil the sit-ins. We, however, learned about the lunch schedule changes from Paul Freeman, a member of the Youth Council who worked as a dishwasher/busboy behind the white lunch counter, and the brother of "sit-inner" Roderick Freeman. We simply started arriving earlier.

On Thursday, August 25, 1960, Mr. Pearson received an anonymous call warning that something would happen to Parker if he continued to participate. I say "anonymous" because Mr. Pearson never told me who called. That was fine, because in this instance I did not have a need to know.

After we arrived at Woolworth, and made our customary purchases at another counter, we proceeded to the lunch counter and sat down. A short time later, a parade of white construction workers walked into the store and stood behind us. Several carried construction-type ropes and large construction tools. They were not there to shop or for take-outs—well, not food anyway. They stood close to the seat where Parker sat, three seats away from me. They did not say a word—they did not have to. They just stood.

I don't recall at any time during the Woolworth sit-in demonstrations seeing police from the City of Jacksonville's police department or patrol officers from the Duval County Sheriff's Department. Despite the constant potential for racial confrontation, and with law enforcement officials' penchant for undercover intelligence during that era, the Jacksonville's police department and the Duval County Sheriff's Office were invisible.

Because of the absence of law-enforcement protection, adults from the NAACP always monitored the sit-ins. We called them "trouble-spotters." We did not have to signal them or say anything. They recognized threats.

When the racial epithet-spewing crowd began to gather alongside the construction workers, our trouble-spotters got in touch with the NAACP office. They knew someone had to do something.

Chapter 8

The Boomerangs

"The power of the white world is threatened whenever a black man refuses to accept the white world's definitions."

—James Baldwin

Several members of the "Boomerangs" walked single-file into Woolworth in a very matter-of-fact fashion and came to the white lunch counter where Parker sat.

The Boomerangs made their way through the crowd of hate mongers and construction workers, and immediately stood behind Parker. We told Parker to go with them, but he insisted he did not want to go. Several of the Boomerangs physically picked him up off the lunch counter seat and eventually persuaded him.

They then formed a circle around him and walked him out of Woolworth onto Hogan Street and away from the store. As they walked Parker away from danger, many in the Woolworth's crowd of whites followed.

The Boomerangs walked Parker down Hogan Street, turning left on Ashley Street. The crowd continued to follow.

When the Boomerangs and Parker got to Clay Street and Ashley Street, which is one block from Broad Street and Ashley Street, they sent Parker on with a couple of Boomerang members and then turned to invite the crowd to continue. The crowd stopped and turned back. The Boomerangs then walked Parker to the Laura Street Presbyterian Church Youth Center. When we later met with Parker, we agreed he would not sit in for a while. It would be an interesting period before we saw Parker again.

White Sit-inner Rescued From White Mob In Jax

Jacksonville citizens who read in Thursday afternoon's local daily paper reports of a group of Negro youths who formed a cordon around a white youth were still puzzled to know the reason for their action.

The real truth which was not printed was this: A mob of whites attempted to molest a white youth who had joined the sit-in demonstrations group and threatened to pull him away from the group.....That is when an "Action Committee" composed of athletic teenagers (not connected with the sit-in group) moved in and defied the agitators to harm the youth and escorted to safety in the colored section.

The white crowd followed to a point.

68

Today, most juvenile delinquent experts would call the "Boomerangs" gang members. After all, they fit all the gang profiles— Black males who lived in a housing project (the Joseph Blodgett Housing project). Arrested for minor fighting skirmishes, they hung out at the Wilder Recreation Park Center in Jacksonville. However, you would not consider the Boomerangs a gang in the traditional sense. They did not have colors, did not carry guns, and did not traffic in drugs as far as anyone could determine. They never resorted to gratuitous violence, though they did fight rivals gangs. You would want any one of them to have your back. They also had tremendous respect for Mr. Pearson and the Youth Council.

The name "Boomerang" resulted from an incident in a local drugstore when some of the Boomerangs "requisitioned" items from the store. Because of the store's layout, you entered one way and exited a separate way. Boomerangs would come into the store and leave quickly. A white employee declared, "They keep coming back just like a boomerang." The name stuck. Of course, the Youth Council never condoned or supported any illegal or violent activity by the Boomerangs.

Many of the Boomerangs were poor. They called Wilder Park and the Wilder Park Recreation Center their home base. Being poor qualified you to live in most housing projects in Jacksonville's Black community. Though we did not realize it or characterize it this way at the time, the housing projects simply "warehoused" poor folk, who in spite of their circumstances, still persevered.

The decorum of all sit-in demonstrations required a steadfast discipline—passive, non-violent resistance. It characterized the civil rights movement in the late fifties and the early sixties. Boomerangs did not join the Youth Council during the sit-ins, though some wanted to join. They made if perfectly clear they could never be a part of a non-violent demonstration. As one Boomerang told me, "If a 'cracker' hits me, I'm going to try and kill him."

As drastic, dramatic and incredulous as it sounds, I believe, as do other Youth Council members, that those construction workers would have tried to lynch Richard Charles Parker that day. We also believe that the Boomerangs saved Parker's life.

Chapter 9

August 27, 1960—Ax Handle Saturday

"There is no medicine to cure hatred."
—African proverb

Mr. Pearson received several calls on the morning of August 27, 1960 about very suspicious and unsettling activities in Hemming Park. He contacted Arnett Girardeau and Ulysses Beatty and asked them to ride with him downtown to Hemming Park.

"As we approached Hemming Park," Girardeau recalled, "we saw several white men wearing Confederate uniforms. Other whites walked around Hemming Park carrying ax handles with Confederate battle flags taped to them. A sign taped to a delivery-type van parked at the Duval and Hogan Streets corner of Hemming Park read, 'Free Ax Handles.' Small fence rails with shrubbery bordered that section of Hemming Park. [As we drove by,] we could see bundles of ax handles in the shrubbery. . . . No one attempted to conceal them.

"We also saw three police[men] separately riding three-wheel police motorcycles. We watched as the police talked to the men dressed in Confederate uniforms. It appeared they were simply having a conversation. Certainly, [the police] were not questioning [the men]. As we circled Hemming Park, the police left."

We arrived at the Youth Center the morning of August 27, 1960 unaware of the Hemming Park activities. We opened our meetings with our usual prayer, not expecting this morning to be any different from other mornings. We sang our usual songs, including "We Shall Overcome." Though our meetings became serious after we started the sit-in demonstrations, this meeting had a more serious bent.

Mr. Pearson explained to us what he, Girardeau, and Beatty saw that morning at Hemming Park. He described the white men wearing Confederate uniforms, and the other white men with Confederate flags taped to ax handles. He told us about the free ax handles sign and warned, "There could be trouble today." Mr. Pearson tried to contact Sheriff Dale Carson to express his concerns, but didn't reach him. Mr. Pearson said he would understand if any Youth Council members decided they did not want to demonstrate that day. We openly discussed our plan of action that day, and whether we would sit in. On the heels of the situation with Parker, we figured we would be facing the Ku Klux Klan in Hemming Park.

Several Youth Council members said we should cancel the day's demonstration. We tried to stay strong and courageous and move forward. Yet a healthy fear of the unknown played a big role in our conversation.

In a recent sermon my pastor, Reverend Rudolph W. McKissick Jr. defined "healthy fear" as knowing the seriousness of your situation, which is an appropriate characterization of how we felt that day. In that same sermon, he defined determined courage as continuing forward even as healthy fear tries to hold you back.

Sometimes, when you face a situation like that the Youth Council faced that Saturday, you rein in the impetuosity of youth. Sometimes, the situation tests youthful mettle and resolve. Fear on one hand, and our interpretation of courage on the other, played a big part in whether or not we would demonstrate. I cannot really say what won the most points to demonstrate. Appropriately, we made our final decision after Mr. Pearson led us in prayer. We always joined hands and prayed at the beginning and the end of all Youth Council meetings. After the prayer that ended our meetings, we would say, "Together we go up, together we stay up"! Corny sounding perhaps, yet the times dictated we do everything in our power to reassure each other and reconfirm our faith in God.

After prayer, I took the first of only two votes by Youth Council members on whether or not to demonstrate. We voted unanimously to demonstrate. Our determined courage overcame our healthy fear. However, instead of sitting in at Woolworth, in front of Hemming Park, we decided to sit in at W. T. Grant Department store, three blocks away from Hemming Park at the corner of Adams Street and Main Street.

After the vote, there were 34 demonstrators, including Arnett

Girardeau. Though he was older than most Youth Council members were, we decided to select Arnett as the sit-in captain because of our view that Arnett could better handle an awkward situation, if one occurred. No one quarreled with his selection.

The W. T. Grant Department store had a lunch counter, though it was not nearly as large as the one at Woolworth. Like Woolworth, Grant also had a "colored lunch counter." When we walked into Grants, I remember seeing four police officers directing traffic at the corner of Main and Adams—or so it appeared to me.

After we sat at Grants white lunch counter, store officials summarily closed and turned out the lights—every one of all.

When we came out of Grant's, and turned west on Adams, we could see in the distance a mob of whites running toward us. As the mob got closer, it became obvious they were swinging ax handles and baseball bats. In a surreal scene, they swung those ax handles and baseball bats at every Black they saw.

It is amazing what the mind's eye captures during tense split seconds of confrontation. I remember seeing a television reporter or a camera operator from local television station Channel 12 on top of a car taking pictures—until someone knocked him off the car with an ax handle.

Employees of stores along the block started locking store doors. If you were inside a store, you stayed inside; if you were outside a store, you could not get in. We had tried to prepare for most scenarios during sit-in demonstrations, but nothing prepared us for an attack as vicious as this.

Although we would laugh later about trying to be cool while looking at those attacking us with ax handles and baseball bats, surviving the onslaught became our primary concern. Most people have held or felt a baseball bat, but not an ax handle. Ax handles usually are as heavy as a baseball bat and can inflict as much damage. They are made of solid wood sturdy enough to hold an ax, and you never forget its look in the hands of someone trying to maim you.

All of us started running and trying to protect ourselves, but Black downtown shoppers were simply no match for those wielding the baseball bats and ax handles. Some fought as best they could, but most simply tried to run for safety.

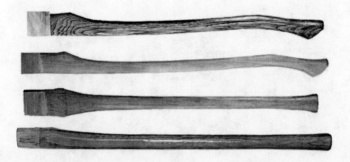

Ax handles are hefty pieces of wood that come in various sizes, weights, and lengths, and must have a sturdiness to handle the axes. Ax handles also come in a variety of lengths, typically from 32 to 36 inches for 3- to 6-pound axes, and can be straight or curved.

In its September 12, 1960 issue, *Life* magazine captured the most vivid image of the attack's aftermath. Several whites are shown attacking Charlie B. Griffin, a friend and a classmate who graduated in 1961 from Northwestern Junior Senior High School. The picture, though in black and white, graphically shows Charlie in his blood-drenched shirt standing next to a law-enforcement official.

Charlie played high school football at Northwestern and, given his size could have ably defended himself in a fair fight. But Charlie became another victim of the racial attacks in downtown Jacksonville that day. The attack on Charlie, it so happened, occurred while he was SWB (Shopping While Black). He was not a member of the Youth Council and was not "sitting in" that day. He would later tell me that as he walked downtown, "this white guy" ran toward him and took a swing at him with an ax handle. When Charlie started to defend and protect himself, more whites came to hit him with ax handles. The attacks against Charlie and other Blacks that day were vicious and cowardly.

As for me, I ran to Main Street first, which is away from the mob, and then north on Main Street to wherever I thought I could find safety. We were on our own—we had no police protection. All law enforcement officers had disappeared.

Afterwards, we came to believe that the Jacksonville Police

Department and the Duval County Sheriff's Department knew in advance that racial violence would occur on August 27, 1960.

As I ran down Main Street, a woman stopped in her car, picked me up, and drove me to the Youth Center . To this day, I cannot remember her face, although Mrs. I. E. "Mama" Williams would later tell me she had been the one to pick me up. I just remember the person asking me if I was hurt and telling me she was a member of the NAACP.

RACIAL FURY OVER SIT-INS

For two weeks Negro sit-in demonstrations had been proceeding quietly in Jacksonville, Fla., but when a white N.A.A.C.P. member joined in, the segregationists' resentment burst into violence. A mob composed largely of rowdies and farmers from across the nearby Georgia border prowled downtown Jacksonville, attacking Negro pickets with fists and often with ax handles. Even casual Negro passers-by (*above*) found themselves in danger.

Responsible Negro leadership immediately suspended all sit-ins. But for two days bands of retaliating Negro toughs roamed through the city, committing vandalism, firing guns at autos and hurling fire bombs into white stores. The toll: 105 arrested, more than 50 injured.

RESCUED BY COP, Charlie Griffin (shown in picture at top) had his head bashed by an ax handle.

Forty years later, I would find out how much Jacksonville and Duval County law enforcement knew about what would happen that day. I met Clarence Sears, an FBI informant with the Ku Klux Klan during the period leading up to Ax Handle Saturday, at the 40th year Ax Handle Commemorative Anniversary Program at Bethel Baptist Institutional Church.

Grateful Acknowledgments to

Dr. Chester A. Aikens

Ford, Jeter, Bowlus, Duss & Morgan, P.A.

Historic Bethel Baptist Institutional Church

The Jacksonville Historical Society

Wendell P. Holmes, Jr.

Willard Payne, Jr.

Gertrude H. Peele

Presentation Resource

The National Conference for Community and Justice
(NCCJ) Jacksonville Region

St. Johns River City Band

Fred W. Schultz

Traditions Restaurant

THE 40TH ANNIVERSARY

OBSERVANCE OF
"AX HANDLE SATURDAY"

Saturday, August 26, 2000
10:00 a.m.

Historic Bethel Baptist Institutional Church
Hemming Plaza
Historic Snyder Memorial

Sponsored By

The Jacksonville Historical Society

The Jacksonville Human Relations Commission

The Jacksonville Urban League

NAACP, Jacksonville Branch

The National Conference for Community and Justice (NCCJ)

"Ax Handle Saturday"
Observance of 40ᵗʰ Anniversary
Saturday, August 26, 2000
10:00 a.m.

Commemorative Mass Meeting
Historic Bethel Baptist Institutional Church

Presiding	Rodney Hurst, Sr.
	President, Jacksonville Youth Council NAACP, 1960
Opening Prayer	Reverend Rudolph McKissick, Sr.
	Senior Pastor, Historic Bethel Baptist Institutional Church
Greetings from the City	The Honorable Matthew Carlucci
	Council Vice President, City of Jacksonville
Presentation of Proclamation	The Honorable Pat Lockett-Felder
	Council Member District 7, City of Jacksonville
Recognitions	Rodney Hurst, Sr.
Statement of Occasion	Rodney Hurst, Sr.
Interpretative Dance "Revelation"	Attitudes Performing Arts Studio
	(as performed by the Alvin Ailey American Dance Theatre)
"Lift Every Voice and Sing"	Choir & Assembly
by James Weldon Johnson (1871-1938)	
Benediction	Reverend Rudolph McKissick, Sr.
	Senior Pastor, Historic Bethel Baptist Institutional Church

Commemorative Walk
Historic Bethel Baptist Institutional Church
to Hemming Plaza

Continuation of the Commemorative Mass Meeting
Hemming Plaza

Presiding	Alton W. Yates
	Vice President, Jacksonville Youth Council NAACP, 1960
Statement of Occasion	Alton W. Yates
Laying of the Wreaths	
Honoring Rutledge Pearson	Mary Ann Pearson & Wendell Holmes Jr.
Honoring Earl Johnson	Janet Johnson & Dr. Arnett Girardeau
Announcement of Historical Marker	William H. Jeter, Jr.
	Immediate Past President, The Jacksonville Historical Society

Continuation of the Commemorative Mass Meeting
Historic Snyder Memorial

Statement of Occasion	Alton W. Yates
Greetings from NCCJ	Scott S. Cairns
	Board Chairman, The National Conference for Community & Justice (NCCJ)
Roll Call, NAACP Youth Council Members, 1960	Rodney Hurst, Sr. & Alton W. Yates
Introduction, Keynote Speaker	Honorable William H. Maness
	Judge (retired)
Keynote Speaker	Honorable Leander J. Shaw, Jr.
	Justice, Florida Supreme Court
Closing Comments	Isaiah Rumlin
	President, NAACP Jacksonville Branch

RECEPTION IMMEDIATELY FOLLOWING PROGRAM AT
TRADITIONS RESTAURANT, 400 N. HOGAN ST.
Buffet Lunch Available for Small Cost
Everyone is Welcome

I did not know Clarence Sears at the time, but he painted a very descriptive timeline of the events leading to Ax Handle Saturday. His CI (Confidential Informant) nickname was Charlie.

Sears gave his report to his FBI manager, who in turn gave the report to Sheriff Dale Carson, or, to be accurate, put his report on the sheriff's desk. Supposedly, a police officer in the sheriff's office intercepted the report and gave it to the head Klansman, a so-called Cyclops. Sears said the report caused quite a commotion at the next Klan meeting. The

Klan realized, according to Sears, that there was "a traitor in our midst," but never knew his identity. According to Sears, the Klan intended the attacks to spark a citywide racial riot. Sears went on to say the Klan met in the Mayflower Hotel the week of Ax Handle Saturday to map out a strategy. Sears also said he purchased some of the ax handles from Sears Department Store in downtown Jacksonville.

During the attacks on us, one could easily have imagined a chaotic scene at the Laura Street Presbyterian Street Youth Center, but Reverend Miller and Mr. Pearson kept everyone as calm as possible. Mrs. Williams put me out of the car at the Youth Center and said she would drive back downtown to find other Youth Council members.

Parents of Youth Council members rushed to the Laura Street Presbyterian Church Youth Center. Unfounded rumors about the attacks downtown fueled fear and anxiety. We received reports of persons beaten to death, but they turned out not to be true; we also heard of shootings, which also were not true. If someone concocted a rumor, we heard it that afternoon. We briefed parents as much as possible on what had happened. Some Youth Council members had not returned to the Youth Center. Despite their obvious concern, not one parent said they regretted their son or daughter sitting in. They reiterated—sometimes emotionally—their support for the Youth Council and the sit-ins.

Word quickly spread to the Black community and Ashley Street about Youth Council members and Blacks beaten downtown. In a matter of minutes, it seemed, a "security force" of Blacks made their way to downtown Jacksonville to protect the Youth Council members and other Blacks downtown. Organized in part by the Boomerangs, the crowd moved from the Joseph Blodgett Homes project, and gathered support moving along Ashley Street. Leaving Ashley Street with substantially increased numbers, Blacks headed downtown.

Richard McKissick, whom many called the "Black Mayor of Ashley Street," managed the Strand and the Roosevelt movie theaters on Ashley Street and ran the day-to-day operations of both theaters. National Theater Enterprises owned the theaters (and two drive-in theaters, the Skyview and the Moncrief), which were under the general management of Arvin K. Rothschild. Rothschild, who was Jewish, actively supported the NAACP. Clint Ezell, who was non-Jewish white, served as Rothschild's assistant.

On Saturdays, according to McKissick, he would unlock one theater for staff preparations and then walk the one block or so to unlock the other theater, also for staff preparations, between 10 a.m. and 10:30 a.m. Both theaters opened for business at 12 noon.

However, when he arrived this Saturday, August 27, 1960 to open the theaters, he said he could sense an unusual tenseness in the air. In his brief walk from one theater to another, several Blacks came to him with various rumors about something happening, or about to happen, downtown. They had seen whites in Confederate uniforms in Hemming Park passing out ax handles, they said.

McKissick said that he then talked with Ezell, who also heard rumors of racial disturbances. Ezell appeared very uncomfortable. They discussed whether to close the two theaters. McKissick said a few minutes after 11:30 a.m., rumors began to escalate about "something happening downtown." Blacks from the Ashley Street area were continuing to congregate, and would shortly make their way downtown. He and Ezell decided to close both theaters and Ezell left for home.

McKissick stayed at the Strand Theater and walked outside, where he saw an unusual number of Blacks milling about on Ashley Street. Within minutes of locking the Strand, bands of Blacks started running toward Ashley Street from downtown, police sirens wailing close behind. Sensing trouble, McKissick reopened the Strand to allow approximately a dozen or so Blacks to come in and hide upstairs in the Strand balcony. After locking the theater again, he said he stood outside to watch. Shortly thereafter, police on motorcycles stopped one block away at the corner of Broad Street, dismounted, and started walking down Ashley Street. They apparently intended to make arrests, because a police paddy wagon accompanied them.

They patrolled both sides of Ashley Street, stopping and looking in stores and businesses. They also looked in the alleys between the stores on Ashley Street. Questions about who they were looking for or what happened went unanswered. According to McKissick, he continued to stand outside the Strand in his manager's attire (suit and tie) until the police passed the Strand. He said they asked him if there were persons in the theater. "Absolutely not," he said, in what he calls one of the biggest lies he ever told in his life. They were now stopping and frisking every Black male. McKissick still did not know what had happened downtown but word slowly began to circulate throughout Ashley Street that whites were attacking Blacks downtown and that a race riot "was going on downtown." Many white store owners on Ashley Street closed their stores and left for the day.

After spending almost two hours there, the police finally left Ashley Street sometime between 2 p.m. and 3 p.m. Ashley Street was a main thoroughfare to the Interstate system, and traffic picked up again—whites started driving through Ashley Street heading toward the Interstate. Blacks started stoning their cars. Police quickly returned to Ashley Street with a cordon of police cars some 20 to 30 strong, sealed it off, and shut it down. Bullhorns screeched as law enforcement officers told everyone to get off the street. They arrested those who did not immediately move, including Black store owners. By 6 p.m., McKissick said, Ashley Street was shutdown and dark. Convoys of law enforcement vehicles patrolled from downtown to the Ashley Street area. Today you would call it a total lockdown.

When whites attacked Blacks that day, no law enforcement officials or law enforcement vehicles were visible anywhere in the downtown area. But as scores of Blacks later made their way to downtown Jacksonville to protect other Blacks and defend themselves where necessary, Jacksonville Police Department vehicles and Duval County Sheriff Department cars seemingly came from everywhere. They closed off downtown Jacksonville. The situation had quickly changed from no police or sheriff's officers to scores of law enforcement officials everywhere.

Reverend Wilbert Miller stood no more than five feet five inches tall, but he stood seven feet tall that Saturday when a Duval County Sheriff patrol officer tried to come onto the property of the Laura Street Presbyterian Church, ostensibly to "interrogate" some Youth Council members. The officers had no warrant, or even an explanation.

Exerting pastoral authority, Reverend Miller would not allow the patrol officer—or anyone, for that matter—talk with anybody on the Laura Street Presbyterian Church property. Emblazoned in my mind is the sight of Reverend Miller, with all of his five-foot-five-inch stature, looking up into the eyes of this patrol officer, who stood at least six feet tall, and telling him not to set one foot on the church's property. The patrol officer left.

79

White Mob Is Seen Weilding Axes, etc.

Two ax-armed men are seen. Note policeman

Youth holds sign that rephrases NAACP

Youth Council members, ministers, parents, community leaders, and other Blacks started arriving at the church and the Youth Center. Youth Council members who participated in the sit-in that morning were finally returning to the Youth Center.

When Reverend J. S. Johnson arrived, he immediately gathered everyone on the porch and sidewalk of the Youth Center. Reverend Johnson then offered one of the most stirring prayers I have ever heard. You do not judge a prayer or the person praying, but even at age 16, you know a mighty prayer when you hear it.

Reverend Johnson asked Youth Council members to understand that God was still in charge and would not allow anyone to "turn us around." God took us "to the hills and the valleys," he said, concluding with his famous line that the "die was cast." We sang "We Shall Overcome," and the tears started to flow.

As Mr. Pearson, Marjorie, and I along with other Youth Council members left Laura Street Presbyterian Church later that afternoon, everything appeared to move in slow motion. Even the air seemed to hang heavy. For the first time in my life, I felt real tension. One of the Boomerangs came by and yelled, "Mr. Pearson, you and Rodney better put some black shoe polish on your face or something." We laughed. He might have been trying to be funny, or he might have been deadly serious. Being light-skinned that day would be a liability he seemed to suggest.

Later, some Blacks and whites would blame Ax Handle Saturday on the Youth Council NAACP because we dared challenge apartheid, American-style by demonstrating at white lunch counters. If we had just tucked our tails between our legs and danced a few doo-dahs, things would be just fine—the racial peace and tranquility that Blacks and whites had grown to love so much in Jacksonville could still manifest itself in the community.

The paradox is so overwhelming. Here is a country based on the Christian ethic of loving your fellow man and embracing Jesus Christ. Here is a country that which primarily uses the teachings of Jesus Christ as the center of its religious life. Here is a country that on every Sunday morning reads countless biblical verses that speak of love. Yet, here is a country throwing those very teachings and its accompanying love out the window, violently attacking young Blacks for pursuing their God-given and constitutionally assured rights. Here is a country that blames those same Black young people for instigating the violence of which they were the victims.

Racial riots are ugly. They are community wars. They crystallize man's contempt for his fellow man based on skin color. Historically, race riots usually involve white Americans unilaterally exacting violence on Blacks. It is an obvious by-product of racism and blatant discrimination. However, the violence that resulted from Ax Handle Saturday literally traveled a two-way street.

Later that same day as violence spread throughout the community, white radio station announcers were imploring their white listeners to "stay out of Black neighborhoods" and Black radio station announcers were imploring their listeners to "stay out of white neighborhoods." The warnings applied especially to insurance agents, domestic workers, gardeners, store owners, laundry and dry cleaner delivery people, and the drivers of all delivery and furniture store trucks. Unfortunately, some did not get the message in time. Many Black and whites were beaten, or worse, that day, that evening, and that night because they were in the wrong place at the wrong time.

An interesting story made its rounds late on the evening of August 27, 1960 and throughout the following week. Until recently, I felt we had reliable information sources, yet I never tried to verify the story's accuracy until I started writing this book. According to Daddy K, one of the original Boomerangs, Klan members decided they would ride into the Joseph Blodgett Homes Housing Project located one block away from Springfield. Springfield was an all-white neighborhood at the time. The Blodgett Homes were an all-Black housing project. Only the wide expanse of a recreation park and two city streets separated the two communities.

Late in the evening of August 27, 1960, a well-armed truck full of purported Klan members rode into the Blodgett Homes area near the Jefferson Street swimming pool. The residents were waiting. According to King, persons in the truck fired at apartment units in the Blodgett Homes; Blodgett Home residents returned the fire from relatively close range. The truck then sped away.

But later that night, rocks and Molotov cocktails hit whites driving Interstate 95 near Black neighborhoods. Blacks who drove close to white neighborhoods had their cars fired upon and stoned.

Chapter 10

Mrs. Ruby Hurley

"We have a powerful potential in our youth, and we must have the courage to change old ideas and practices so we may direct their power toward good ends."
—Mary MacLeod Bethune

Prior to Ax Handle Saturday, Mr. Pearson kept NAACP Field Secretary Bob Saunders and NAACP Regional Director Mrs. Ruby Hurley informed daily about our sit-in activities. Saunders and Mrs. Hurley made regular reports to Gloster Current, the director of NAACP Branches at the National NAACP Office, and to Roy Wilkins, National NAACP Executive Secretary.

Mr. Pearson's telephone calls to Saunders and Mrs. Hurley on August 27, 1960 gave them a blow-by-blow account of the ax handle attacks downtown. Both Mrs. Hurley and Bob Saunders immediately made plans to come to Jacksonville. Saunders came in from a conference in Augusta that evening, and Mrs. Hurley flew in from Atlanta the next morning.

A major racial disturbance, certainly one of the magnitude of Ax Handle Saturday, would bring national, regional, and state NAACP staff to a community to help the local NAACP branch, youth council, or college chapter coordinate activities. As the nation's oldest civil rights organization, the NAACP was organized to provide that assistance. One reporter warned that NAACP bigwigs would come into town to run things. *Ah, the interpretation of the press!* For the record, local NAACP officials always made the decisions, in consultation with national NAACP staff.

Mr. Pearson picked up Mrs. Hurley from the airport Sunday morning and brought her directly to Dr. Henderson's house. Mrs. Hurley would stay in the home of Mrs. Mildred Smith, a Black female who owned an exquisitely manicured bed and breakfast, which she called Avondale.

With few high-quality segregated hotels and motels in Jacksonville, Black bed and breakfast homes similar to Avondale were a necessity in the days of segregation. Black celebrities and public personalities simply did not have anywhere else to stay when they visited a Black community. Therefore, before visiting Jacksonville, you placed a telephone call to Mrs. Smith to check Avondale availability and to notify her when you would arrive. Pictures of many noted entertainers such as Duke Ellington, Cab Calloway, Billy Eckstine, and the Ink Spots adorned the walls of Avondale.

Mrs. Ruby Hurley, Southeast Regional Director NAACP

Legendary in the struggle for civil rights, Mrs. Ruby Hurley was born in 1909 in Virginia. Her work as a civil rights activist began in 1939, serving on a committee that successfully fought to get renowned Black singer Marian Anderson space to perform in concert when Ms. Anderson was banned from segregated Constitution Hall in Washington, D.C., by the Daughters of the American Revolution.

In 1943, Walter White appointed Mrs. Hurley Youth Secretary of the NAACP. Under Ms. Hurley's leadership, the number of NAACP youth chapters expanded from 86 to more than 250, and to a total membership of 25,000. Thus, she began a career devoted to the fight against racial injustice that would span more than four decades.

In a civil rights movement largely dominated by men, her significance as a female official in the NAACP and as a woman of color, became most noteworthy. In addition to her work as an administrator, Ms. Hurley played a dominant role at the grassroots level of the movement, investigating racially motivated crimes, including the murder of 14-year-old Emmet Till.

* * *

Because of threats against the NAACP local office and the office's visibility, Dr. James Henderson, a successful Black dentist and businessman in Jacksonville, invited us to meet at his home in Magnolia Gardens. Dr. Henderson's house became our temporary "command post." A volunteer security squad called the Loyal Sons and Daughters, watched Mr. Pearson's house that night.

Ms. Hurley arrived at Dr. Henderson's house, and we continued mapping out our actions for the next few weeks. She did not walk in, as the NAACP Southeastern Regional Director, to plan for us; she helped us plan. More importantly, as a confident civil rights veteran of many racial crises, she just knew what to do. She instilled a confidence in us that both reassured us and motivated us.

I marveled at the brain trust that had hunkered down with us. Mrs. Hurley, Bob Saunders, Earl Johnson, and Mr. Pearson kept Dr. Henderson's home telephone busy. They took calls from the media all over the country. They made calls to Roy Wilkins, and other NAACP officials. They received calls from Roy Wilkins, and other NAACP officials. Earl Johnson discussed legal strategies with the NAACP and with NAACP Legal Defense Fund lawyers, and even talked with Thurgood Marshall, the Fund's head. I talked to the press, and to Roy Wilkins. There were no cell phones in those days, and many busy signals.

Those at Dr. Henderson's house the night before and that morning also included Mrs. Geneva Henderson (Dr. Henderson's wife), Mrs. Janet Johnson (Earl Johnson's wife), Marjorie Meeks, Alton Yates, and John Henry Goodson (NAACP Adult Branch President). There were many others: Youth Council members; Dr. Henderson's neighbors, who doubled as security; NAACP officials; and well-wishers, who were everywhere, both inside and outside the house. We later joked that if someone had planted a bomb in Dr. Henderson's house, it would wipe out half the civil rights movement brain trust in Jacksonville and the Southeastern Region.

Jacksonville's Youth Council NAACP, made up of junior high school students, high school students, college students, and young adults, had just experienced a civil rights lifetime in a couple of weeks. Notwithstanding the steady hand of Mr. Pearson's leadership, Mrs. Hurley gave all of us a morale boost. She certainly boosted Youth Council members and immediately assumed the position of our "adopted mother."

As we discussed our next strategy moves, especially whether we wanted publicity, Jacksonville moved to the national stage of civil rights.

We called a press conference late that morning at Dr. Henderson's house to discuss some of the plans we would later present at the NAACP mass meeting.

Some members, of the press, already in town because of the earlier sit-in demonstrations, and some national press who hurriedly came to Jacksonville because of the riot, found their way to Dr. Henderson's house.

As the press arrived, several reporters wanted to take pictures of Dr. Henderson's house as the press conference location. We would not let them take the pictures—if you like, call it paranoia. Today, you probably would not have a press conference at someone's home after a major racial riot, but, then again, it was a different day, and his neighborhood, as we would later learn, could probably defend itself more effectively.

We certainly did not want to expose Dr. Henderson and his neighborhood to potential violence. Rumors about what the Ku Klux Klan would do were all over the place. However, Dr. Henderson and his neighbors demonstrated that they could protect themselves. They certainly had the firepower. Thank God, they did not have to use it.

When the press conference began in Dr. Henderson's living room, Mrs. Hurley read a prepared statement and announced some of the action that we would propose taking in the mass meeting later that day at St. Paul AME Church. St. Paul was located on the corner of 13th and Myrtle, one block from New Stanton Senior High School and two blocks away from Isaiah Blocker Junior High School. That fact was not lost on me that day.

Chapter 11

August 28, 1960—the day after Ax Handle Saturday

"There is no easy walk to freedom anywhere, and many of us will have to pass through the valley of the shadow of death repeatedly before we reach the mountaintop of our desires."

—Nelson Mandela

Despite all the racial furor of the previous day, the *Florida Times-Union* had nothing on the front page of its August 28, 1960 newspaper about any disturbance. There was nothing on pages 2 through 14, either.

Finally, on page 15, a headline read, "Tight Security Lid Is Clamped on City After Racial Strife." *Tight security?* Where?

The story included no real reporting of what had happened the previous day. No quotes from the NAACP were included in the "coverage". In fact, the NAACP wasn't even mentioned in the article. Obviously, this represented a business-as-usual spin to reassure city residents this little racial skirmish was under control. Yet, a major race riot had started in downtown Jacksonville and spread throughout the city. Jacksonville became a national press story, including a feature story on the Saturday night and the Sunday night network news shows. Police statistics would also belie how the local press downplayed the riot.

The *Florida Times-Union* reported police statistics indicating that "33 Negroes and 9 white persons were arrested on charges ranging from inciting to riot to fighting." The *Tampa Tribune* gave the number of arrests as 85, Negroes and whites. The *St. Petersburg Times*'s figures were 150 arrested and 70 injured. Florida governor LeRoy Collins had the National Guard go on "standby for possible duty if further racial disorders were to break out in Jacksonville." Yet the headline "Racial Strife" suggested a social club disagreement in Jacksonville.

The *Florida Times-Union* article on August 28, 1960 further stated that:

"Mayor Burns called an emergency meeting early yesterday of top police officials to map plans to keep the tense situation under control. Sheriff Dale Carson returned hurriedly from vacationing in St. Augustine to join Burns at the session." The article and the headline were a little at odds as to the seriousness of what had happened.

A smaller article below and on the right of page 15 quoted Luther Reynolds, the chief of police of the City of Jacksonville's police department. Reynolds was quoted as saying: "The question of sit-in demonstrations or integration of lunch counters is subject only to the decision of the store manager. Only he determines whom to serve. Should a merchant choose to ask any person to leave his premises and should such person refuse, then that person is in violation of the trespass law and subject to arrest. Until merchants request police assistance in the removal of a person, there are no legal grounds for police action other than to preserve peace."

In this game of political chess, Chief Reynolds had checked to the stores: the individual store manager—not the police—would decide when a shopper is trespassing; the individual store manager would decide who to serve at a lunch counter. Therefore, the store—not the police—would decide when to arrest Black shoppers.

To us, the statement meant that if we went to one counter and Woolworth accepted our money, we were not trespassing. Yet, if we went to another counter, and Woolworth refused our money, we were trespassing. To us, this strategic yet politically flawed logic almost represented a checkmate.

Remember, James Word, the manager of Woolworth, said they were following Southern laws and traditions. City political leaders and the police deftly shifted the burden of integrating the lunch counters, preserving the peace, and determining whom to arrest to the department store managers. It was hardly reassuring and certainly not in the best interest of the stores bottom line.

In retrospect, given the editorial policy of the *Florida Times-Union* at that time, we were surprised that they even published an article on the riot. A benign neglect mentality—no, total insensitivity—permeated the local media.

I would later discover an interesting memo from Bob Saunders, NAACP Field Secretary, in archived NAACP papers in the Library of Congress. He reported to the National NAACP office that a reliable source from the wire services told him that representatives from one of the daily newspapers called and suggested that the wire services not carry stories on the sit-ins and segregation in Jacksonville. As a result, Bob Saunders set up contacts so that the wire services could receive regular information on developments.

Out-of-town reporters from the *Tampa Tribune*, the *Atlanta Journal and Constitution*, the *Orlando Sentinel*, the *Daytona Beach Morning-Journal*, the *Chicago Tribune*, the *Miami Herald*, and papers in Chicago and New York covered the sit-ins. Readers of their papers knew more about what happened in Jacksonville than those living in Jacksonville.

In numerous conversations over the years, Eric Simpson commented how whites started purchasing the *Florida Star* newspaper to find out what was happening in the movement in Jacksonville. Eric indicated that on several occasions, he had to double and even triple the *Florida Star* print run. At times, segregation had its rewards—even for the Black press.

* * *

Mr. Pearson received a call from Reverend Blaine at St. Paul AME Church, who said the church had received a bomb threat. Reverend Blaine said he was not fearful; he simply "wanted us to know." We did not call the Jacksonville Police Department or the Sheriff's Office. Considering the events of the last 24 hours, we did not trust them. We could not contact the FBI. It was probably just as well because we did not know if we could trust them either.

Members of St. Paul AME Church, members of the NAACP, and others inspected the church that morning for suspicious activity and suspicious items. Rumors were flying that the Ku Klux Klan planned on Sunday to ride down the middle of Myrtle Avenue, in front of St. Paul AME Church. Other groups, including Army veterans, volunteered to stand guard outside the church just in case somebody tried to start something. They were armed.

We spent most of the morning preparing for the mass meeting. Youth

Council members went to Black churches throughout the community, passing out fliers and asking pastors to announce the mass meeting at St. Paul AME Church. The events of August 27, 1960 became the obvious focus of many sermons on Sunday.

The adult NAACP brain trust of Rutledge Pearson, Earl Johnson, Mrs. Ruby Hurley, and Robert Saunders spent the remaining time putting together the resolutions I would read calling for federal investigations of the Jacksonville Police Department and the Duval County Sheriff's Department. We would also initiate boycotts against the *Florida Times-Union* and all downtown department stores. The Youth Council decided to continue sit-ins that following Monday, August 29, 1960.

Prior to the start of the mass meeting, Mr. Sol Silverman of Washington, D.C. asked to meet with the Youth Council. Sent to Jacksonville, Florida by the U.S. Civil Rights Commission, he asked that we not immediately resume demonstrations and observe a cooling-off period. According to Silverman, not resuming the demonstrations would allow the U.S. Civil Rights Commission an opportunity to investigate the actions of the City of Jacksonville, including those of law enforcement officials, while also investigating the circumstances of the attacks on August 27, 1960. The so-called cooling-off period, he said, would also allow Blacks and whites to work on some of the problems related to the sit-ins.

Mr. Pearson left the decision up to the Youth Council. Youth Council members in attendance reluctantly voted not to resume sit-ins on August 29 to allow the requested cooling-off period. A recent book about Jacksonville errantly stated that state NAACP officials came to Jacksonville to call off the sit-in demonstrations. In fact, the Jacksonville Youth Council NAACP voted to discontinue the sit-ins.

Mr. Silverman thanked us "for giving the federal government and the Civil Rights Commission a vote of confidence" and he stayed and attended the mass meeting.

In its August 29, 1960 edition, the *Times-Union* wrongly reported that the Youth Council decided against resuming demonstrations because of fear of continued violence and the City of Jacksonville's newly imposed law enforcement procedures. For this particular story, *Times-Union* reporters never talked with Youth Council members or NAACP officials. They also did not employ any Black reporters who could have helped to report the news.

In fact, the Black press kept its Black readership in Jacksonville and other communities better informed than the white press. In his editorials, Eric Simpson, the editor of the *Florida Star*, seized the opportunity to criticize the *Florida Times-Union* for neglecting to publish news about the sit-ins and other activities leading to Ax Handle Saturday.

* * *

If you were late getting to St. Paul A.M.E. Church for the mass meeting, you had trouble finding a seat. St. Paul had brought in extra chairs from wherever they could get them. They still did not have enough. Of course, the national print press and the national television media were already there. They had set up earlier in the afternoon. The atmosphere in the church was electric. Those of us in the Youth Council, were excited and proud to see a packed church of Black Folk supporting the Youth Council NAACP in our fight for human dignity and respect.

I presided at the mass meeting. As was customary with NAACP mass meetings, we opened with a spirited singing of "Lift Every Voice and Sing" which set the energy level for the evening. Those in attendance wanted and needed to hear the real story of August 27, 1960, as well as the NAACP's plans for future action and future Youth Council demonstrations. It was an event when no one looked at a watch to see how much longer the meeting would last.

Alton Yates and Marjorie Meeks gave the "blow-by-blow" report of everything that had happened the day before.

Mr. Pearson introduced Mrs. Hurley, who delivered an outstanding message. Attorney Earl Johnson, Bob Saunders, and Mr. Pearson all spoke.

When we got to the business portion of the mass meeting, and to the question of whether the Youth Council would resume the sit-ins, I read the following Council statement:

"In view of the violence and rioting in downtown Jacksonville . . . yesterday, the 27th of August, and in view of the mounting movement and reports of impending chaos, vandalism and rioting, the Youth Council of the Jacksonville Branch NAACP has determined not to picket and sit [in] in Jacksonville on Monday. We do not do this out of fear of physical injury, but to allow responsible citizens of the community, colored and white, an opportunity to marshal the forces of reason and common sense, so that peace and order may prevail. If no positive efforts to establish lines of communication between both races are forthcoming in the near future and no steps taken to redress our grievances, we will have no recourse except to resume our demonstration[s]. In the meantime, our efforts will be to initiate a policy of selective buying. We will ask Negroes to refrain from any and all downtown purchases."

NAACP papers
pt 20 reel 6

Mrs. Hurley addressing the August 28, 1960 Mass Meeting (Courtesy Rodney L. Hurst, Sr.).

We were taking this action, I explained, to enable the proper authorities to seek appropriate resolutions to our many grievances.

We also introduced Sol Silverman. He did not speak.

I then read the following resolution, which represented our plan of action for the next few months:

"Whereas, members of the Jacksonville Youth Council National Association for the Advancement of Colored People have protested the exclusion of Negro Citizens from lunch counters at Cohen Brothers,

Rodney L. Hurst Sr.

Woolworth['s], Grant, Kress, McCrorys and Sears Department Stores;
And whereas such demonstrations were conducted in a peaceful and
non-violent manner;

Downtown Store Boycott Urged By Jax NAACP

Selective Boycott Against Stores

The NAACP Saturday called on this city's 140,000 Negroes to join in a full scale selective buying campaign against the entire business district.

Mrs. Ruby Hurley, the Association's south east regional director outlined the local NAACP Youth Council's "don't pay to be segregated" project at an enthusiastic mass meeting.

It was held at St. Paul AME Church, on Myrtle avenue at 13th street and was sponsored by the Jacksonville NAACP Youth Council. The Council has proven a major stabilizing force in this hate – ridden community of high racial tensions.

Violence flared here Saturday, August 27, when 300 white men and boys, armed with baseball bats and ax handles, attacked peaceful and orderly NAACP Youth demonstrating against lunch counter bias as nearby police turned their heads.

Mrs. Hurley called for the turning in of all Cohen Brothers Department store charge cards saying "white businessmen in this city must learn once and for all that they can no longer collect the Negro's cash in one hand—while slapping him with the other."

Negroes represent one-third the total population of Jacksonville and surrounding Duval County. Cohen's has stubbornly refused to serve Negro customers at lunch counters.

Mrs. Hurley cited the success of similar selective buying campaigns in Savannah, Ga. and Nashville, Tenn., both of which have about the same proportion of Negro populace.

The NAACP executive also criticized the "biased editorial policies of the Jacksonville Times-Union and Journal" terming their reportorial activities "among the most unprofessional I have seen in my 18 years in the field of race relations."

She then called for the Negro community to cancel all subscriptions and all newstand purchases, pointing out that both publications have their circulations verified by the Audit Bureau of Circulation an independent agency.

"If Negroes in Jacksonville and other parts of the state stop buying these two newspapers, their circulation rates will soon show an appreciable drop. In turn, this will affect their advertising revenue.

"No Madison Avenue advertising agency or state advertiser wants to insert advertising lineage in a media that is losing its pulling power," she asserted.

NAACP Urges Selective Buying Drive in Jacksonville

'Don't Pay to Be Segregated'

JACKSONVILLE.—The National Association for the Advancement of Colored People has called on this city's 140,000 Negroes to join in a full-scale selective buying campaign against the entire downtown business district.

Mrs. Ruby Hurley, the association's Southeast regional director outlined the local NAACP Youth Council's "don't pay to be segregated" project at an enthusiastic mass meeting.

It was held at St. Paul AME Church on Myrtle Ave. at 13th St, and was sponsored by the Jacksonville NAACP Youth Council.

VIOLENCE FLARED here Saturday, Aug. 27, when 300 white men and boys, armed with baseball bats and ax handles, attacked NAACP youth demonstrating against lunch counter bias—as nearby police turned their heads.

Mrs. Hurley called for the turning in of all Cohen Brother's Department Store charge cards saying "white businessmen in this city must learn once and for all that they can no longer collect the Negro's cash in one hand—while slapping him with the other."

Negroes represent one-third of the total population of Jacksonville and surrounding Duval County.

Cohen's has stubbornly refused to serve Negro customers at its lunch counters. It has been the site of consistent sit-ins by the NAACP Youth Council since Aug. 17.

IT WAS ALSO among stores congratulated in a three-column, full page advertisement in the Jacksonville Chronicle for resisting "sit-in demonstration attempts here in Jacksonville."

A recent advertisement was paid for by the White American Christian Patriots of Duval County. The Chronicle is one of the leading news organs of the White Citizen's Councils in Florida.

Other Jacksonville stores "congratulated" included McCroy's, Kress', Grant's, Sears-Roebuck, Morrison's Cafeteria and Woolworths.

MRS. HURLEY cited the success of similar selective buying campaigns in Savannah, Ga., and Nashville, Tenn, both of which have about the same proportion of Negro populace.

The NAACP executive also criticized the "biased editorial policies of the Jacksonville Times-Union and Journal," terming their reportorial activities "among the most unprofessional I have seen in my 18 years in the field of race relations."

She then called for the Negro community to cancel all subscriptions and all newsstand purchases, pointing out that both publications have their circulations verified by the Audit Bureau of Circulations, an independent agency.

• If Negroes in Jacksonville and other parts of the state stop buying these two newspapers, their circulation rates will soon show an appreciable drop. In turn, this will affect their advertising revenue.

•

"No Madison Avenue advertising agency or state advertiser, wants to insert advertising lineage in a medium that is losing its pulling power," she asserted.

Mrs. Hurley concluded by reminding her audience of the three-year period that it took for commerce in Little Rock to resume its preschool integration conflict norm, after the September, 1957 outburst.

And, whereas responsible Negro Citizens made attempts to contact Judge Marion Gooding, Mayor Haydon Burns[,] and Police Chief Luther Reynolds for the purpose of obtaining adequate police protection against imminent conflict from certain violent and irresponsible elements of the citizenry; Be it resolved, that the members of the NAACP Youth Council and the Negro Citizens of Jacksonville call upon the Justice Department of the United States to investigate fully the brutal attack by an organized mob on peaceful and law abiding citizens, whose only purpose at the time was demonstrating against racial discrimination under the protection of the United States Constitution.

"We also call upon the Justice Department to investigate the failure of law enforcement officers of Jacksonville [and] Duval County to provide adequate protection for law[-]abiding citizens who were attacked by the mob which assembled with bats, [a]x[-]handles, and clubs in full view of law enforcement officers.

"Be it also resolved that we call on Negro [c]itizens and other sympathetic citizens of this community to continue to protest against all forms of racial discrimination in businesses operating in this community.

"We also call upon the [m]ayor of the City of Jacksonville to appoint a group of citizens representing a cross[-]section of the City of Jacksonville[,] who will work on a Bi-Racial Commission to seek ways of solving the various problems which exist in the City of Jacksonville. Such a committee should be organized as recommended by the [g]overnor of the State of Florida earlier this year.

"Be it further resolved that we call upon the [p]resident of the United States, Dwight David Eisenhower, to investigate the denial of civil rights to Negroes in the City of Jacksonville, State of Florida, and that the presidential candidates of both political parties openly voice their sentiments against mob action and that they . . . seek to put into effect those positions of their respective party platform, which endorse attempts by Negro Citizens to end racial discrimination at lunch counters and in employment.

Respectfully submitted,
The Jacksonville Youth Council NAACP
Rodney Hurst, President"

Rodney L. Hurst Sr.

We addressed the resolution to:
The Honorable Dwight David Eisenhower
President of the United States

The Honorable Senator John F. Kennedy,
Democratic Candidate for President of the United States

The Honorable Vice President Richard M. Nixon
Republican Candidate for President of the United States

U.S. Attorney General Herbert Brownell

NAACP Papers pt 20 reel 6
Library of Congress

After I finished reading the resolutions, the meeting erupted into thunderous applause and choruses of "amens." If not for the excitement of the moment, tears would have certainly flowed from my eyes. I asked for a motion from the floor and for unanimous support to adopt the resolution. Those attending the mass meeting stood and overwhelmingly adopted the resolution.

Many attendees remarked that, for the first time in their memory, Jacksonville's Black community was truly united. The national press accurately captured a large portion of the mass meeting. In fact, in these days before CNN news, and other 24-hour news giants, Jacksonville became the lead story on the late night network news. Most news stories usually received a 30-second sound byte, or maybe a minute. Jacksonville frequently received more time. In fact, for several days, Jacksonville and Ax Handle Saturday became the lead national news story of the civil rights movement.

I kept looking to see if any members of the Boomerangs were in church that day. I knew some were outside "guarding" the church because the Klan had issued its threat. I did not see any Boomerangs inside the church—initially—but they were there. They were all sitting in church respectfully dressed in their shirts, ties, Botany 500 suits, and Stacy-Adam shoes. This meeting was a first for many of them.

16-Year-Old Youth Heads Jax NAACP Youth Activities

JACKSONVILLE, Fla. — When you heard he was only 16 years old and you knew that he was the guiding hand in one of the smoothest protest maneuvers you've seen yet and you see the sound, sensible, highly intelligent statements coming from his lips, you realize there must be something unusual about Rodney Hurst, president of the local NAACP Youth Council.

There is.

For he is also guiding a dedicated group of high school and college students, some of whom are students at some of the nation's leading colleges and university. Yet he is only 16. Now you know, for sure, that age has no monopoly on wisdom. Rodney Hurst proves it—at 16.

Rodney is a handsome lad with a bit of fuzz under his chin, and a general assortment of freckles. He was graduated last June from Northwestern High School, where he didn't play football, basketball or other such sports.

■

HE WAS MORE the literary type, with a yen for journalism.

RODNEY HURST
... 16-year-old leader

That, naturally, gave him a probing mind. He was advertising director and reporter on his school newspaper. He plays tennis and softball, so don't think he isn't inclined towards athletics. It's just that he has had other things on his mind.

When he was 13, Rodney joined the NAACP Youth Council. Last September they elected him president. It was a terrific choice, as developments have shown. Rodney is not from a wealthy family or home. In fact, he's from a broken home. His mother and dad are separated. His mother is a secretary at a hospital. His dad is a waiter at a local hotel. He lives with his mother and she is proud of him.

When Rodney worked as a busboy at Cohen's store cafe, he observed many things around him—the menial jobs for Negroes, among them—and they had an effect on him. It helped shape his thinking, and his desire to do something to change things. The NAACP Youth Council was a good vehicle to do that job. The youngster is devoted to it, and has worked arduously for its programs.

Hurst believes in systematic planning, and in doing one thing at a time, doing it well. That was reflected in the decision three months ago when the first "sit-in" failed at Kress' store.

■

PLANNING AND research to know the strong and weak points of the enemy was in the young leader's m i n d. Perhaps, we should not use the term "leader" to describe him, but call him director-spokesman. "There is no leader," he says. "There are many who lead, with each doing his job in his own particular area." He explains this:

He has had help from Jacksonville students who are home from such schools as Howard University, Langston, Morehouse, University of Pittsburgh, Morris Brown, FAMU, Southern, Grambling and the local Edward Waters College. These youths represent fine minds and they have poured their thinking into the big plan.

WHERE IT STARTED — Palm-lined Hemming Park in Jacksonville, Fla., is where the mob of young white hoodlums gathered on Aug. 27 to begin their wanton attacks upon Negroes. Facing Woolworth's the mob swung their axe handles and baseball bats from this point, while police stood by and did nothing. Ironically, the Negro student "sit-ins" were NOT in Woolworth's but in Grant's, some distance away, at the time. Also, the "sit-inners" were not involved in the riots. — Anderson Photo

'Action Committee' Forms Cordon

Youths Protect White Friend

(Courier Press Service)

JACKSONVILLE, Fla.—When a mob of whites tried to grab a white youth who was "sittin-in" with Negro student protesters here, an "Action Committee" of Negro teen-agers not connected with the "sit-in" formed a protective cordon around the white youth and escorted him to safety in the Negro section.

The white youth was later identified as Richard Parker, a student at Florida State University and a native of Indiana.

He was arrested by police later and charged with vagrancy, although he told the judge he had over $200 in the bank and didn't need to work. The judge found him guilty, charged him with inciting the Negro protest and gave him a stiff jail sentence and fine.

Meanwhile, the 350-member Duval Classroom Teachers Association, in a formal meeting, went on record pledging full support to the "sit-ins" and picketing by the NAACP Youth Council.

In another aside, the local Trailways Bus station quietly integrated its restaurant in keeping with a directive issued several weeks ago at Petersburg, Va., headquarters of the cafe chain.

Chapter 12

Richard Charles Parker II

"A life is not important except in the impact it has on other lives."

- Jackie Robinson

I asked several Youth Council members and Boomerangs if they had seen Parker. We had not heard from him since Thursday of that week. I wondered if he had gone back to Florida State. In the days to follow, we learned that police had begun surveillance on Parker the day he sat in with the Youth Council NAACP.

Law enforcement officials were absolutely convinced that Parker was either the sit-in leader or an NAACP leader. On the day following the riot, Parker was in a white downtown restaurant. Though he was merely sitting and drinking a cup of coffee, the police came into the restaurant and arrested him.

Parker was charged with a myriad of offenses, from "inciting to riot" to "vagrancy," though he was a student at Florida State University, had approximately $30 in his pockets, and had a local bank account with $200. According to the press and court documents, Municipal Judge John Santora asked Parker if he "was one of the persons leading the riots?" and why he did not "remain in Massachusetts," where he belonged?

When Parker answered that he was a proud member of the NAACP, Judge Santora interrupted him and sentenced him to 90 days in jail, simply because he could.

Later that day, police and jail officials told jailed whites Parker was a leader of the NAACP, and they promptly attacked him.

We did not know of the police arrest of Parker until the week following Ax Handle Saturday. Based on a tip from a jail trusty, attorney Earl Johnson went to the Jacksonville city jail to visit Parker. Police initially denied Parker was an inmate. When Mr. Johnson demanded to see Parker, they changed their story.

Mr. Johnson then learned of Parker's injuries. When Mr. Johnson asked Parker about them, he found out that white inmates had attacked Parker, broke his jaw in two places, and dislocated his shoulder. According to Parker, the police and jail officials watched as the attack took place. After the jail's medical staff wired his jaw shut because of the fractures, he received little follow-up medical attention. Jail officials also served him regular solid food, which he obviously could not eat. Attorney Johnson asked Parker if he "could mash soft [food] or liquefy [it] enough to suck [it] through a straw." Parker told him no. Parker also told him they would not even give him a straw to suck water.

Mr. Johnson demanded that officials at the Jacksonville city jail and the Jacksonville Police Department serve Parker milk. Jail officials responded by saying they could not provide special consideration to inmates, and the jail's budget did not allow milk.

When Judge Santora sentenced Parker to 90 days in jail for vagrancy, pandering, trespassing, and anything else it appeared that would stick, he also fined Parker $500.

Jacksonville Police Chief Luther Reynolds and Judge John Santora would not see Mr. Johnson to discuss Parker's case. With the help of the NAACP, Mr. Johnson first went through the state court system seeking legal relief for Parker. The NAACP continued to demand the jail provide medical relief for Parker. Several days later, jail employees served Parker milk and a doctor finally treated his injuries.

Weeks went by and the filing of many legal briefs by Attorney Johnson and Attorney Shaw. The NAACP appealed the case and Judge Santora's decision to the Florida State Supreme Court who denied the appeal. That irony is not lost on me today since Attorney Leander Shaw would become the first Black appointed as Chief Justice to the Florida State Supreme Court.

In the meantime, sympathizers from all over the United States sent Parker letters, money, and books. When the NAACP, Attorney Johnson and Attorney Shaw sought redress in federal court, and with protests mounting throughout the country, the case was miraculously resolved. Parker still spent 60 days in jail, however, of a 90-day sentence. The NAACP paid Parker's fine, which the court reduced from the original five hundred dollars. After his release from jail, Parker left Jacksonville and went to Nashville, Tennessee where he was one of a number of students arrested for participating in a sit-in demonstration there.

Later, when Parker attempted to re-register at Florida State University, the college's disciplinary committee denied his application, according to R. R. Oglesby, dean of students. Oglesby never gave a reason.

Parker Needs Cash, Books

White Sit-In Denied Freedom in Florida

JACKSONVILLE, Fla.—The Florida Supreme Court, at Tallahassee, has refused to free Richard F. Parker, a white student who is serving a 90-day sentence for taking part in "sit-in" demonstrations here during August.

Parker sits in jail with a broken jaw received when he was slugged by a segregationist after the riots which followed the sit-ins.

Unable to eat solid food, he lost 25 pounds during the first 35 days he was imprisoned. Because of his belief in the philosophy of non-violence, Parker refuses to prosecute his attacker.

THE STUDENT'S attorneys plan to appeal to the Federal courts to release Parker. They contend that his sentencing on a vagrancy charge violates his rights under the First, Fifth and 14th Amendments to the U. S. Constitution.

Parker himself points out that he was in no sense a vagrant. He had funds in a local bank, was on vacation as a student from Florida State University, Tallahassee, and had a room in a local hotel when arrested.

Jacksonville police admit they arrested Parker when he was sitting alone in a white restaurant waiting for a cup of coffee. They had been watching him for 10 days because he was the only white person who had the courage to join Negro students in sit-ins.

The student's jaw was shattered and several teeth knocked out. His mouth is still wired up and he is unable to eat anything but food in liquid form. However, his spirits are good and he has been strengthened in his belief that he is doing right.

"I've always felt this way," he said. "I've always had a feeling for the Negroes. I've always thought they were not given rights they were entitled to as American citizens."

TWO NEGRO attorneys here are contributing their services in efforts to free Parker.

They feel that if his conviction is allowed to stand, it will constitute a threat to other sit-in participants in Florida and throughout the South.

These lawyers are Earl M. Johnson, 410 Broad St., Jacksonville, to whom funds may be sent to help in processing an appeal for Parker.

Parker himself needs books to read and money with which to buy extra milk. He also needs letters of encouragement from people who believe in him. His address is Duval Country Jail, Jacksonville, Fla.

He will be there until the end of November unless the courts heed his plea for freedom.

Richard Parker Free But Goldfinch Isn't

Fla. State Youth Released Following Storm of Protests

■

JACKSONVILLE, Fla. — The power of concerted protest was shown, again, Oct. 27, when authorities, here, released Richard Frank Parker from jail, after he had served 60 days of a 90-day sentence.

● Parker, a white student at Florida State University, Tallahassee, was jailed Aug. 23, for taking part in sit-in demonstrations, sponsored by Negro youths.

He and his attorney, Earl M. Johnson, attributed his early release to protests which descended upon city officials after it became known that Parker was in jail with a broken jaw, received when he was hit by a segregationist.

■

SYMPATHIZERS from all over the United States sent him money and books. With the extra funds, he purchased milk which enabled him to gain back some of the weight he lost in the early days of his confinement.

He had been unable to eat solid foods, because of his jaw fracture.

Parker, who plans to re-enter F.S.U. if they'll accept him, said he received about 20 letters per day, during the latter part of his stay in jail. He said:

"I feel good, and I want to thank all the people who supported me, and backed me. I plan to, and will, continue to participate in demonstrations against segregation. My time in jail has not decreased my dedication to this cause at all."

Tulane U. Student Faces 10 Years in Prison for 'Sit-In'

■

NEW ORLEANS, La. (ANP)— S. Langston Goldfinch, a white student at Tulane University, faces a possible 10-year prison term for joining Negro students in a sit-in here.

● He was charged with criminal anarchy, under Louisiana's sedition statutes, after his arrest at McCrory's lunch counter, Sept. 17.

Goldfinch is charged, also, with criminal mischief and conspiracy to commit criminal anarchy. Freed under $2,750 bond, he awaits arguments, Nov. 3, on the constitutionality of the charge of criminal mischief.

■

HEARINGS HAVE not been set on the anarchy charges, which were filed, despite the voiding of state sedition laws by the U. S. Supreme Court in 1956. Courts in Massachusetts, Kentucky and Louisiana, later, dismissed sedition indictments as a result of the U. S. ruling.

● District Atty. Richard Dowling said he based the anarchy charges on a statement by Goldfinch when he was arrested. Officers said he told them: "I have come here for a purpose, and I will not leave until I have accomplished that purpose, or have been arrested.

● Goldfinch explained, later,

Milk Gives Strength to 'Sit-In' Pals

PORT ORANGE, Fla. — "Will you Drink-In for Freedom? . . . You may have wanted to join a Sit-In, but have not had the opportunity to do so. Now you can join a Drink-In."

This was the invitation sent by Mrs. Don Calhoun and Mrs. William McMillan for an interracial "dinner" party in Daytona Beach, Fla.

Guests were asked to contribute a dollar for the defense of Richard F. Parker, the white Fla. State University student who was jailed in Jacksonville, after taking part in Negro demonstrations there.

THE "DINNER" consisted of milk only—hence the name, Drink-In—because Parker himself was living on milk after his jaw was broken by a segregationist fellow-prisoner.

Besides giving the guests an opportunity to identify with Parker's sacrifice, the "milk-only" meal proved to be an easy and

that his purpose was to buy a cup of coffee, but Dowling interpreted his statement as a threat against the state of Louisiana.

The student, who is doing graduate work in philosophy, was sitting with three Negro students when arrested—one from Xavier University, one from Dillard University and one from Southern University, New Orleans branch.

Chapter 13

Dr. Martin Luther King

*"Those who profess to favor freedom, and yet depreciate
agitation, are men who want crops without plowing up
the ground."*

—Frederick Douglass

Dr. Martin Luther King Jr sent a telegram late Saturday afternoon after
the news had broken on national television about Ax Handle Saturday.
He told us "violence was not the answer" and that if we needed his
help, we should contact him. Unfortunately, his telegram implied that
the Youth Council NAACP had joined in the violence—that Youth
Council were the ones brandishing the ax handles. Dr. King should
have known that as he dealt with inaccurate news stories nationally,
we constantly had to deal with inaccurate news stories about the civil
rights movement in Jacksonville.

This is one reason why the Black press, nationally and locally, was
so vitally important during that phase of the civil rights movement in
Jacksonville. They reported the news based on what happened and did
not try to slant the coverage.

In his telegram, Dr. King had asked if we needed his help, though
he knew, as most people did, that Jacksonville was an NAACP city.
You have to understand the time. Civil rights leaders and organizations
did not just show up in your city if you were experiencing a racial
issue or situation. You invited them to come and assist you if you
needed their assistance. Civil rights issues could always use support
from the local and the national community, but the NAACP did not
need someone outside of its organization to come into a city to take
charge.

As the oldest civil rights organization in the country, with arguably
the most effective civil rights organizational structure and the largest
membership, the NAACP did not ask for nor did it need leadership

assistance. In fact, most civil rights organizations usually asked the NAACP for *its* assistance.

In what I can best describe as a collaborative response by Johnson, Mrs. Hurley, and Mr. Pearson, with some input from me, we answered Dr. King's telegram for John Henry Goodson, the president of the Jacksonville NAACP Adult Branch, and to whom Dr. King had addressed his telegram. Our response in its entirety follows:

Rev. Martin Luther King Jr.
Ebenezer Baptist Church
Auburn Avenue Northeast
Atlanta, Georgia

Dear Rev. King:

We deeply appreciate your offer of assistance. We too abhor violence. We reject violence as a way to achieve any of the objectives which we, and other fair-minded people, seek for all Americans without regard to race, creed or color. In rejecting violence, however, we do not deny, but instead re-affirm the rights of individual and collective self-defense against unlawful assaults.

The NAACP policy over the years has supported exercising the right of defense as in Elaine, Arkansas in 1919; the Sweet Case, in Detroit, in 1925-26; the Columbia, Tennessee violence, in 1946, and in many other cases.

The NAACP youth members here demonstrated peaceably for two weeks in an effort to obtain lunch counter service. On the day in question, when armed white mobsters attacked our youth and other innocent bystanders, Negro youth and adults behaved with marvelous and Christian restraint. Their exemplary conduct, however, did not prevent beating[s] by police officers and use of unwarranted force in making arrests. Our lawyers are defending those arrested[,] including [one] courageous white member who was subjected to heavy penalty and brutally beaten in jail.

We have called on our people to observe law and order working within duly constituted means of legal redress. Our youth are courageous, but not bitter and are determined to resolve this conflict by obtaining justice through the use of proved and demonstrably successful techniques.

There had been no call to arms or unlawful assembly and there will be none on the part of the NAACP. Lieutenant Crews, head of the Police Intelligence Squad, has stated that disturbances here have been caused by gangs known to the police for two or three years. However, we have made contact with many of their leaders to get their cooperation in keeping peace.

The Negro in the South has suffered long enough and in Jacksonville we are observing a temporary truce, to permit restoration of order and further considerations of our requests. But, should an honorable settlement not be offered, we intend to press harder for our objectives using peaceful and legal means. Since the violence that has erupted is not NAACP violence, and since our people are alert and responsible, we believe we are fully able to meet whatever situation . . . may arise.

Thank you for your prayers and moral support.

Yours Sincerely,

J. H. Goodson

President

Jacksonville Branch NAACP

> NAACP papers,
> Pt. 27 sec. A, reel 3,
> Library of Congress

In other words, without meanness, and without non-Christian indifference, we established and maintained the rules of engagement in the civil rights movement. Dr. King's telegram simply misidentified the situation and some of the issues in Jacksonville. However, the fact that Dr. King asked if we needed his presence certainly meant that Jacksonville had caught the attention of the country and the national spotlight.

Dr. King never visited Jacksonville in connection with the sit-in demonstrations, and we never asked for his help. We did not blame Dr. King for his telegram. In fact, Mr. Johnson, Mr. Pearson, and Dr. King would later spend many, many hours together during the 1964 racial conflicts in St. Augustine, Florida.

Many persons apparently underestimated the maturity of the Jacksonville Youth Council NAACP because of the name and because college students and NAACP college chapters were involved in most sit-in demonstrations. Our organizational title did not imply college students. News references and Dr. King's telegram implied that Youth Council members did not have the world experience necessary to decorously conduct sit-in demonstrations.

Dr. King never apologized for his telegram. He did not have to apologize. He sincerely sought to help. He legitimately thought that Youth Council members were somehow involved in and responsible for initiating the violence. Although the Jacksonville Youth Council membership roster consisted mostly of high school students, we understood the importance of the movement, and of our actions. Moreover, we considered the struggle for human dignity and respect too important to lose by violently reacting to those whose hatred had permeated their thinking, their lives, and even their very souls.

Chapter 14

The First Kneel-in

God gives nothing to those who keep their arms crossed.
- African Proverb

When the Youth Council decided to worship at a predominantly white church, we chose Alton Yates, Jacquelyn Stephens, Marjorie Meeks, Betty Harper, Mary Alice King, and me as the worshippers. We felt it fitting to worship at Snyder Memorial Methodist Church.

Reverend Robert Gisler, the pastor of the Snyder Memorial Methodist Church, actively supported the creation of a bi-racial committee, so we wanted to worship at his church.

When Blacks worshipped at heretofore-segregated white churches, the press designated the event as a "kneel-in." [In fact, the press used the "in" for all direct action activities: sit-ins (lunch counters and restaurants), kneel-ins (churches), wade-ins (swimming pools and beaches), and lay-ins or sleep-ins (hotels and motels).]

Morning worship had already begun when we arrived at Snyder Methodist Church. We waited for Reverend Gisler to complete his prayer. We entered the church and sat in seats near the front. I could hear audible gasps and some expressions of exasperation from church members. Reverend Gisler graciously welcomed us. The remaining church service was pleasant yet tense.

Shortly after we arrived, Japhus Baker walked in with his camera. Japhus worked for the *Florida Star* and had an excellent reputation as a photojournalist. Japhus knew about the planned kneel-in that morning at Snyder Memorial Methodist Church, but we did not invite him nor did we know he would come to the church as a reporter with his camera. Of course, he had no need to clear his working assignments with us.

Tall and considered handsome by many females, especially those in the Youth Council, Japhus had an additional professional dimension.

Though Black, he looked white enough to pass as white. He never did, but he could have done so at any time. He had naturally straight hair and very fair skin. In the Black community, fair-skinned Blacks were commonly described as "high yellow." Japhus definitely fit the description. My good friend Willard Payne, a native of Houma, Louisiana would say the boy could pass both the comb test and the paper bag test.

When Japhus covered news and community events for the *Florida Star*, including several racial events, he was a white journalist simply doing his job.

So get the picture—several Blacks kneeling at the church's prayer railing for the first time, in a segregated white church, a few days after Ax Handle Saturday in downtown Jacksonville. In walks a photographer with his camera, who then takes a picture of us in church.

To say that taking that picture created a commotion is a great understatement—all hell broke loose. Reverend Gisler promptly declared from the pulpit that no one could take pictures during a worship service in Snyder Memorial Methodist Church. Another parishioner exclaimed loudly, "That's it!" I had no idea what he meant but quickly imagined. Several white male members of the church leaped to their feet, grabbing Japhus and his camera. Church members confiscated his camera and film, and ushered him out of the church. Eventually, he did get his camera back.

I would like to think that nothing else would have happened to Japhus if Snyder's congregants knew he was a Black journalist, though nothing else happened to him as a white reporter.

In his closing remarks, before final prayers and benediction, Reverend Gisler said, "We knew you were coming, but we did not know when."

After church adjourned, we shook hands with several church members and Reverend Gisler. They greeted us very warmly. Frankly, we expected they would. We left as soon as possible. We never took part in another kneel-in.

Chapter 15

The NAACP Mass Meetings

"We should emphasize not Negro History, but the Negro in history. What we need is not a history of selected races or nations, but the history of the world void of national bias, race hate, and religious prejudice."
—Carter Woodson

If you wanted to know what was happening in the civil rights movement in Jacksonville in the late fifties and early sixties, you attended an NAACP mass meeting.

Jacksonville Youth Council NAACP mass meetings were civil rights movement revivals. Mass meetings energized, re-energized, motivated, inspired, and kept you spiritually driven while giving you updates on civil rights activities locally and nationally.

Mrs. Ruby Hurley Speaker
At NAACP Mass Meeting

Mrs. Ruby Hurley, Southeast regional director of the NAACP will be the main speaker when Jacksonville's N.A.A.C.P Youth Council holds its weekly mass meeting at 3:30pm Sunday in St. Paul A.M.E Church, Myrtle Avenue and 13th. Street.

Rodney Hurst, president of the local youth council stated that one important phase of Sunday's session will be the kick-off preliminary to the annual membership drive for both youth and adult councils.

Program participants will include Robert Saunders, state NAACP field director, Alton Yates, who will deli-

ver a youth council progress report, George Putson, in a vocal number and Rutledge Pearson who will introduce the main speaker.

Mr. Hurst in commenting on the over-capacity at t endance which has attended the youth council's first two mass meetings, wishes to thank the general public for their admirable support of the council's program.

Mass meetings also represented the non-sophisticated yet effective communications network of the Movement.

We always gave weekly progress reports on our efforts downtown, updating the status of the "selective buying program," the status of the bi-racial committee, the overall status of the Youth Council NAACP and the NAACP generally, and of course civil rights developments throughout the country.

Our selective buying campaign in downtown Jacksonville represented another weapon to fight segregation. If store owners and managers wanted to maintain their segregated practices, we wanted them to feel it in their profit margin.

By all accounts, we were accomplishing our goals with the selective buying campaign. However, because the struggle goes beyond waiting to see what would happen, we decided to increase the pressure on downtown stores by adding an ingredient for the Black community, to drive the point home. To reinforce our serious resolve to keep Blacks from shopping downtown and even out of downtown altogether, we sent members of the NAACP Adult Branch and the Youth Council NAACP downtown on a regular basis to take the names and the pictures of Blacks who continued to shop downtown. Some folks were upset, but "freedom is not free," and Blacks really needed to understand that. We read their names at our mass meetings, and the *Florida Star* published their pictures. We reinforced the seriousness of our efforts downtown. There were some Black shoppers downtown—not many—but we sent a message the business community received loud and clear.

Then there is "Lift Every Voice and Sing."

One of the reasons "Lift Every Voice and Sing" is so important to the civil rights movement is the poignancy and relevance of its lyrics. At a time in this country when lynchings of Blacks happened as often as the weather changed, James Weldon Johnson penned words that captured the resolve of Black Americans and our continued faith in God. As much as the public considered "We Shall Overcome" the civil rights movement's signature song, those in the movement considered this mighty hymn one of motivated inspiration.

Take the words of the third verse, for instance:

God of our weary years,
God of our silent tears;
Thou who hast brought us thus far on the way;
Thou who hast by thy might, led us into the light,
Keep us forever in the path, we pray.

Lest our feet stray from the places
Our God where we met thee
Lest our hearts drunk with the wine of the world we forget thee
Shadowed beneath thy hand
May we forever stand
True to our God
True to our Native land. Amen.

From "Lift Every Voice and Sing"
By James Weldon Johnson

Asked to speak at an Abraham Lincoln birthday celebration in Jacksonville, James Weldon Johnson wrote a poem instead of speaking. With time running short, plans changed again, and James asked his brother, music teacher John Rosamond Johnson, to help him write a song. James Weldon Johnson recalled that near the end of the first stanza, when the following two lines came to him, "the spirit of the poem had taken hold of me":

Sing a song full of the faith that the dark past has taught us.
Sing a song full of the hope that the present has brought us.

Later, James Weldon and John Rosamond sent the song to their New York publisher, but thought little more about it. However, the public found it hard to forget. Children in the South, and eventually all Blacks throughout the United States, continued to sing it. "The lines of this song repay me in elation, almost of exquisite anguish, whenever I hear them sung by Negro children," James Johnson wrote in 1935.

James Weldon Johnson always referred to "Lift Every Voice and Sing" as the Negro national *hymn* and not the Negro national anthem, as most of us do. Julian Bond, in the book *Lift Every Voice and Sing: A Celebration of the Negro National Anthem 100 Years, 100 Voices*, writes about how Johnson, through his lyrics, proclaims his unswerving self-confidence and optimistic faith in African Americans, and his strong belief that the then existing system, a counterfeit representation of the United States Constitution, could not endure. Sociologist E. Franklin Frazier pointed out that in "Lift Every Voice and Sing," James Weldon Johnson gave the African-American struggle for freedom a certain nobility and purpose. In the 1920's, the NAACP adopted "Lift Every Voice and Sing" as the Negro national hymn.

What a mighty God-inspired pen James Weldon Johnson wielded! Not many know that Johnson, a native of Jacksonville, wrote this great hymn while in Jacksonville, Florida. John Rosamond Johnson, James's brother, was on the faculty of Florida Memorial College. Florida Memorial College, located at that time in Jacksonville, held regular classes at Bethel Baptist Institutional Church. According to local historians, Mr. Johnson could have written "Lift Every Voice and Sing" at Bethel Baptist Institutional Church.

(I am especially reminded of the civil rights movement whenever I hear Bethel Baptist Institutional Church's mass choir, under the directorship of Maestro Omar Dickenson, singing a variation of Roland Carter's arrangement of "Lift Every Voice and Sing". OK, it is a shameless plug).

Our mass meetings continued every Sunday at churches throughout the Black community.

One of our more memorable mass meetings occurred when NAACP Executive Secretary Roy Wilkins addressed a packed St. Paul AME Church on Sunday evening, December 18, 1960.

Mr. Wilkins coming to Jacksonville gave a new energy to those of us involved in the civil rights struggle for human dignity and respect in Jacksonville.

NAACP SAYS STAY OUT DOWNTOWN

NAACP Secretary Coming For Rally

★ FLORIDA STAR ★

And NEWS Vol.10-No.59 Saturday, December 17, 1960 - Jacksonville, Florida

Top NAACP Leaders Spark Sunday's Mass Meeting Here

Mounting interest is being manifest here concerning the Sunday night public mass meeting appearance here of Roy Wilkins, executive secretary of the National Association for the Advancement of Colored People and other top leader strategists of the organization. Program gets underway promptly at 9 p.m. in St. Paul A. M.E. Church, Myrtle and 13th.

Sponsored by the Jacksonville Branch NAACP Youth Council, it has also been announced that Mrs. Ruby Hurley, the NAACP's Southeastern Regional director and Robert Saunders of Tampa, the organization's state director will enhance the program, according to Rodney Hurst, youth council president.

The sponsors feel that the appearance here of top NAACP leaders is both timely and advisable. It is realized that the veteran internationally known civil rights leader has a wealth of knowledge and experience in combating the barriers confronting second class citizens, a local organization spokesman stated.

"Mr. Wilkins guidance and advice is urgently needed by all minority group members whether they're part of our organization or not," the spokesman added. "It is pertinent that we draw upon this wealth of expert advice from the top man in this field," the

Roy Wilkins
...here Sunday

Six Sit-Ins Convictions Are Upheld

TALLAHASSEE-The City Court convictions of six Florida A and M University students charged with disorderly conduct during sitins here were upheld Wednesday following an appeal to Circuit Judge Ben Willis' ct.

The students, Vincent Moore, George Carter, Robert Kemp, Benjamin Cowins, Willie Black and William Mathers, had been convicted by City Judge John Rudd and sentenced each to pay a $100 fine or serve 60-days in jail. On charges of unlawful assembly, Cowins, Kemp, Black and Mathes

School Board Plans To Fight Integration

Jax NAACP Youth Council To Continue Counter Sit-ins

Although rumors expected racial violence have been branded as unfounded the NAACP Youth Council has issued an announcement urging Negroes to stay away from downtown.

Throughout the week the FLORIDA STAR has been receiving a number of telephone calls from persons stating they had heard that citizens were being warned to keep away from downtown after Thursday because an outbreak of violence by youth gangs was expected.

A check with various sources revealed that there was no basis for the report that the youth gangs were planning any sort of violence. Another rumor to the effect that St. Luke's Hospital has been alerted to accommodate expected victims of violence was denied by the hospital's director, who, however, said he had heard the rumors of violence.

A Youth Council spokesman said that although the group plans to continue it's sit-in campaign in a peaceful manner and it is very possible that white hoodlums (meaning the rowdy handle brigade that set off the Aug. 27 riots) are planning to attempt to stop them. "Therefore, "he added, "there is always a possibility an outbreak." But such outbreaks could be stopped if the police department would do its job.

It was reported that the Ku Klux Klan will stage a cross-burning and public speaking meeting Saturday night on U. S. Highway 1.

The Jacksonville sit-in movement is part of a campaign through-out the southurging Negroes to curtail Christmas shopping and "Save Your

School Board Seeks Integration Reply Delay

Duval's Board of Public Instruction Wednesday asked the U. S. District Court for a time extension to Jan. 25 in answering the National Association of Colored People's suit seeking integration of public schools here and also has secured-a said to be staunch segregationist-Fred H. Kent as associate counsel to Elliott Adams, school board legal representative in the integration suit.

It was learned that the normal extension time for filing answer to an integration suit is 20-days under federal court ruling. The request for an extension of time by the board of public Instruction was signed by Kent, Adams, and Davisson Dunlap. Kent and Dunlap are said to be affiliated with the Jacksonville law firm of Adair, Ulmer, Murchison, Kent, and Ashby.

Insufficient Time

According to Kent, the 20-day ruling required to answer the integration suit or before Dec. 27 would require a large amount of preparation to be

U. Of Georgia's Registration Quiz Attacked

ATHENS, Ga.—A federal court Wednesday heard Hamilton Holmes, 19, who with a fellow student, Charlayne Hunter is seeking to enter the University of Georgia, testify that university officials asked questions about interracial parties, prostitution, and sit-in demonstrations while interviewing him concerning his application to enter the school.

Holmes stated that he told the interviewers that he had attended mixed social parties, but had not engaged in

Roy Ottoway Wilkins, executive director of the National Association for the Advancement of Colored People (NAACP), was the grandson of Mississippi slaves. Born August 30, 1901, in St. Louis, Missouri, Wilkins dropped his middle name, which was the name of the doctor who delivered him, as soon as he "learned how to write."

Roy Wilkins in conversation with President Lyndon Johnson
(Picture courtesy NAACP Papers, Library of Congress)

Between 1955 and 1977, Wilkins held the positions of executive secretary and executive director, respectively, of the NAACP. Under his leadership, the NAACP campaigned for the Civil Rights Act of 1964, the Voting Rights Act of 1965, and the Fair Housing Act of 1968. He helped organize the 1963 March on Washington, consulted with presidents of four administrations, and received the nation's highest civilian honor—the Presidential Medal of Freedom. Wilkins died four years after his retirement from active leadership with the NAACP, in 1981.

"In each generation, God somehow manages to select someone that has the perseverance, the ability, the articulation to be able to improve upon the contribution that [ethnic groups] can make," said Representative Charles Rangel, New York, discussing a 1984 bill to award a commemorative medal to Wilkins's widow. "As you protect the constitutional rights of one set of people, you're protecting the constitutional rights of all. So, whether we're talking about a black person or white, a Jew or Gentile, a Catholic or Protestant, Roy Wilkins has done so much for America and the free world."

When Mr. Wilkins spoke, people listened. Because he spoke from a national stage, he commanded the attention of the national press.

When you received a telephone message from Roy Wilkins, you always put his name at the top of your callback list, irrespective of your station in life. His mere presence drew attention wherever he traveled. He also had to have protection at the highest level. Whenever Mr. Wilkins came to town, FBI agents monitored his appearances, in part to provide protection, but as we have learned, who knew what FBI Director J. Edgar Hoover had in mind? Of course, many community persons volunteered to protect him.

When he spoke, Mr. Wilkins had a dignified, unconceited swagger that let you know he represented the largest civil rights organization in this country. Once, he jokingly accused me of upstaging him in front of his friends in Virginia. (*See chapter 21*)

After Earl Johnson filed the NAACP school integration suit against the Duval County School Board, Mr. Wilkins addressed the impact of school integration nationally and in Duval County. When Roy Wilkins gave you an update about the civil rights movement, you knew it came firsthand.

A couple of months earlier, Reverend A. Leon Lowry, pastor of the Beulah Baptist Institutional Church of Tampa, Florida and the president of the Florida State Conference of NAACP Branches, spoke to an overflow crowd during a mass meeting held at Bethel Baptist Institutional Church. Eric Simpson, in his October 1, 1960 edition of the *Florida Star*, reported that Lowry spoke to a crowd "of more than 1000 enthusiastic NAACP members and supporters."

Reverend Lowry's civil rights roots went back to his days of teaching theology at Morehouse College in the 1940s. Among his students was Martin Luther King Jr.

It was never about a hot dog and a Coke!

Reverend Lowry led peaceful protests at several Tampa lunch counters in the 1960s and helped found Tampa's first biracial bank. He also helped the president of GTE devise a plan to break down racial barriers at the phone company.

Rodney L. Hurst Sr.

NAACP Mass Meeting Set For Sunday

State NAACP President
Speaks at Mass Meeting Here

One of the leaders who played an important role in the recently successful integration of Tampa's downtown stores eating facilities will be main speaker at the regular weekly meeting of the Jacksonville NAACP Youth Council.

Rev. A. Leon Lowry, state NAACP president will head the council's mass meeting program which is scheduled Sunday, (Sept.25) at 4 p. m. in Bethel Institutional Baptist Church, Orange and Hogan Streets.

Rodney Hurst, president of the local NAACP youth council stated Friday that the dynamic state NAACP president is being brought here to step up the council's selective buying campaign against local department stores practicing bias and racial discrimination.

Hurst also added the group's boycott of dailies which continue to "slant" editorial comment concerning Negroes and refuse to give proper titles to Colored women will also be discussed and stepped up in tempo.

The local president urges all interested persons in Duval to attend this meeting so as to become fully acquainted on t h e progress made by the organization t h us far.

"For that reason," he added, starting time of Sunday's regular weekly meeting has been advanced to 4 p.m. in order that individuals having previous commitments will have an opportunity to attend.

Team captains, groups precinct, area and individual workers are urgently requested to attend the important meeting of this year's annual NAACP Membership drive committee scheduled for 8 p.m. Monday at Elks Rest, 726 W. Duval Street.

Mrs.Queen B.Williams director, in issuing

*Reverend A. Leon Lowry, flanked by NAACP Youth Council members
Herman Grice on the left, and Bill Holton on the right.*

Reverend Lowry became president of the Florida NAACP in 1960, and later became the first Black elected to the Hillsborough County School Board, where he served for 16 years. The Florida Bar awarded him a medal of honor for easing racial tensions and promoting social justice in the Tampa area.

At the mass meeting, Lowry spoke of the Florida State NAACP Conference's support for the effort in Jacksonville, pointing out that because of the Tampa community's cooperation with and support of the Tampa Bi-Racial Committee, eighteen stores in Tampa had peacefully desegregated. Comparing Mayor Burns to Nero, who fiddled while Rome burned, the Reverend Lowry said, "In Jacksonville, while the City of Jacksonville tried to deal with its ever-expanding racial problems, Mayor Burns continued to sit on his blessed assurances."

Many national civil rights dignitaries addressed our NAACP mass meetings. In a follow-up to school integration cases resulting from *Brown v. Board of Education of Topeka*, Mrs. Daisy Bates, another great civil rights stalwart of Little Rock, Arkansas, along with the "Little Rock Nine," spoke to us about the violent confrontation and struggle to integrate Central High School, in Little Rock, Arkansas in 1957 at St. Paul AME Church.

Daisy Bates, second from right in the back row, stands with the students known as the Little Rock 9 (Courtesy NAACP).

It was as president of the Arkansas State conference of the NAACP that Bates coordinated the efforts to integrate Little Rock's public schools after the Supreme Court's Brown v. Board of Education decision outlawed segregated public schools in 1954. Nine African-American students, the "Little Rock Nine," were admitted to Little Rock's Central High School for the 1957-1958 school year. Violent white reaction against integration forced President Dwight D. Eisenhower to order 1000 army paratroopers to Little Rock to restore order and protect the children. Bates was the students' leading advocate, escorting them safely to school until the crisis was resolved.

Father Theodore Gibson (Courtesy Florida Photographic Collection).

Father Theodore Gibson of Miami, President of the Miami Branch NAACP and at the time the president of the Florida State Conference of Branches NAACP spoke to one of our mass meetings about the Struggle and the ongoing investigation of him by the Johns Committee.

After *Brown v. the Topeka Board of Education*, Thurgood Marshall targeted the State of Florida, saying of the state:

"We found not one instance on the part of the political leadership to even consider the possibility of desegregating."

When the NAACP sued the Miami Florida School System, and filed notices of other school integration suits, Florida fought back and formed the Florida Legislative Investigation Committee, nicknamed the "Johns Committee" for its two-time chair and most prominent member, State Senator Charley Johns.

The Florida Legislative Investigative Committee. Chairman, and former Governor Charley Johns, is shown wearing glasses, in the left foreground (Courtesy Florida Photographic Collection)

A former Ku Klux Klansman, staunch white supremacist, and former Governor of the State of Florida Charley Johns, and the Johns Committee proceeded to spend more than four years harassing officers of the NAACP. Ostensibly, the Johns Committee was intended to keep subversive state groups in check. In reality, the FLIC functioned as a conservative weapon to stifle civil rights activism in Florida by attempting to expose the state NAACP as a Communist-front organization, and the committee made Miami's NAACP branch its primary target. In 1957, FLIC witch-hunters began a six-year crusade in Miami to "show a definite tie-up between the Communist movement and the NAACP" in Florida. *Florida Historical Quarterly, the Robert W. Saunders Papers, Steven F. Lawson, "The Florida Legislative Investigation Committee and the Constitutional Readjustment of Race Relations, 1956-1963.*

Of course, they never found any link between the NAACP and Communism.

By the mid-1950s, Florida segregationists, like those throughout the South, had come to see anticommunist rhetoric as a potential means to forestall civil rights gains for blacks. According to guardians of white supremacy, any group that challenged the established order was dangerously un-American.

After the Johns Committee found Father Gibson in contempt for not turning over the NAACP membership list, and pressed for the enforcement of contempt charges, it eventually secured a jail sentence and hefty fine against Gibson. With their insistence on sending Reverend Gibson to jail, however, the Johns Committee had inadvertently set in motion another of the NAACP's famous Supreme Court battles. Reverend Gibson won a stay of sentence and, with the help of Thurgood Marshall and other NAACP attorneys, took the case all the way to the U.S. Supreme Court. In 1963, the court ruled in Reverend Gibson's favor, exonerating him of all charges and setting an important precedent for the freedom of association.

NAACP Field Secretary Robert Saunders, who became NAACP field secretary after Harry T. Moore, also spoke at our mass meetings, as did NAACP Southeastern Regional Director Ruby Hurley. We also featured local persons, including Earl Johnson, Mr. Pearson, Youth Council Secretary Marjorie Meeks, Youth Council Vice President Alton Yates, and me.

Jacksonville NAACP mass meetings were literally civil rights history in action.

Chapter 16

Reverend Charles White McGehee

"Our whole constitutional heritage rebels at the thought of giving government the power to control men's minds."

—Thurgood Marshall

Few white ministers in Jacksonville Florida supported the Youth Council NAACP and the sit-in movement in 1960. Reverend Charles White McGehee did as the pastor of the Unitarian Universalist Church in Jacksonville. As did Episcopal Canon Robert McCloskey, Congregational minister Reverend Al Dentler, Reverend Albert Kissling of the Riverside Presbyterian Church, perhaps the dean of white ministers in Jacksonville at that time, and Episcopal priest Father Edwin Harvey.

Canon McCloskey's support and Father Harvey's support were notable considering the conservative philosophy of the Episcopal Church at that time.

In 1959, Father Edwin Harvey contacted Mr. Pearson and suggested a meeting with Youth Council NAACP members and students from Ribault High School, which at that time was all white. We could pick the location. Just a simple sit-down meeting so we could get to know each other, yet a daring statement. Father Harvey understood the consequences, and so did Mr. Pearson. In 1959, Black folk and white folk, irrespective of age, simply did not talk…about anything.

We chose St. Stephens AME Church. Father Harvey agreed and brought a group of 12 students from Jean Ribault High School to meet with members of the Youth Council NAACP at St. Stephens AME Church. The meeting had to occur at night. There were no other options during that time. The fact that we met is quite remarkable in itself. The fact that we met at St. Stephens AME is also remarkable. We found that even with our physiological and cultural differences, we were a lot the same. It certainly was a first time experience for two groups of teenagers, one Black and one white, sitting in a room just talking. Yet, we were establishing lines of communications.

I first met Reverend McGehee in the late fifties when several members of the Youth Council, including Mr. Pearson, and me attended a Unitarian Church service. Isaiah Williams III and Quillie Jones, who were both members of the church and members of the Youth Council, invited us. Reverend McGehee, the minister of the Unitarian Church, came into the service on crutches.

Rev. Charles McGehee (Courtesy Bob Irwin)

A few years later, I would meet Reverend McGehee again at St. Paul AME church in the Mass meeting after Ax Handle Saturday. Oddly, he again had crutches. I would later learn that because of pending spinal fusion surgery, Reverend McGehee had to decide if he would sit in a wheelchair, or stand on crutches, for the rest of his life. His surgery would permanently contour his back. He chose to stand, which spoke volumes about his courage and his character.

When his wife Jeanne, drove him to various functions and meetings, the back of their van was situated in a way so he could lie at an angle. After he was assisted out of the van and onto his crutches, he would make his way to the function, where he would stand. At NAACP Mass meetings, you could always find Rev. McGehee somewhere near the front of the church standing on his crutches. Many times, he was the only white person in attendance.

He courageously and consistently supported the Youth Council and the sit-in demonstrations. For several months, both Rev. McGehee's home and the Unitarian Church building needed to be guarded around the clock by church members because of the McGehees' and the congregation's participation in Jacksonville's civil rights movement.

These ministers did not sit-in or carry a picket sign, nor did they have to, but they would call Mr. Pearson or me at various times with much-appreciated words of encouragement. With all the negatives we endured from the white community, their words spoke loud enough for us.

Chapter 17

Judge Marion Gooding

"I am determined to teach our children the truth about being Black, being Christian, and being faithful to a God who came into history on the side of the oppressed!"
—Dr. Jeremiah Wright

In August 1960, Marjorie Meeks, then Youth Council NAACP secretary, and I enrolled at Edward Waters College.

We both had graduated from Northwestern Junior-Senior High School with excellent grade point averages and scored high enough on the standardized twelfth grade placement examination at the time to become members of the "400 Club" (out of a possible 498). Marjorie had close to a straight-A average. Voted "Most Likely to Succeed," she should have been the valedictorian of our class.

Edward Waters College (EWC), the oldest private college in the State of Florida, is a four-year, liberal arts, coeducational HBCU (Historically Black College and Universities) affiliated with the African Methodist Episcopal (AME) Church. Founded in 1866, and located in Jacksonville, it is named after Bishop Edward Waters, the third Bishop of the AME Church. Yet, EWC is so much more than just historical fact. As an institution of higher education, Edward Waters College, like other HBCUs represents the future for many Black students.

Most Historically Black Colleges and Universities offered student scholarships through the College Intercollegiate Examination Board (CIEB) examinations. Because of my CIEB test scores, several HBCUs offered me a scholarship covering tuition and board.

My first choice was Hampton Institute (now Hampton University) in Hampton, Virginia. Most of the other HBCUs I wanted to attend were also out of the state. Unfortunately, because my mother could not afford the cost to send me away to college, I could not accept any of the out-of-state scholarships. I really wanted to attend Hampton, but subconsciously I also wanted to stay in Jacksonville to continue working with the Youth Council NAACP.

Edward Waters College offered me a scholarship and filled a tremendous need for my family and me, just as it does for many students today.

Prior to the start of the 1960 academic year, EWC President William Stewart received a call from Jacksonville Mayor Haydon Burns, who asked if I had submitted an application to attend Edward Waters College. When President Stewart confirmed that I had and that he had offered me an academic scholarship to attend, Mayor Burns reminded President Stewart that the City of Jacksonville contributed $25,000 to Edward Waters College, and that Duval County gave Edward Waters College $50,000. Of course, at the same time, the City of Jacksonville was contributing $50,000 to Jacksonville University, and Duval County contributed $100,000. Mayor Burns told President Stewart that if I attended EWC, both contributions could be in "serious jeopardy."

President Stewart took my application and Marjorie Meeks's application to faculty members to explain the circumstances and to ask for their support.

Throughout the South, elected officials exerted tremendous pressure on many trustee boards and college presidents of Historically Black Colleges and Universities to expel "student agitators," and to fire faculty members if they participated in or supported sit-in demonstrations in their community.

Interestingly, Edward Waters College hired several new faculty members that academic year fired by their previous institutions under considerable political pressure because those faculty members supported sit-in demonstrations. Many HBCU saw a wholesale reduction in credentialed faculty because members had dared support the challenge against segregation. These were credentialed faculty whom they could ill afford to lose. Nevertheless, racist and intimidating Southern politics demanded their firing.

The telephone call from Mayor Burns to President Stewart continued the Southern strategy of trying to shut down or seriously handicap sit-in demonstrations by any means necessary.

The faculty overwhelmingly accepted the applications from Marjorie and me. President Stewart told us at the time that he would not have rejected our applications, but he wanted the faculty apprised of the situation and the threat.

On December 8 of that same year (1960), I was in class when I received a message to report to President Stewart's office. When I arrived there, two detectives from the City of Jacksonville's Police Department had a warrant for my arrest "for contributing to the delinquency of a minor."

Judge Marion Gooding, a Juvenile Court Judge for Jacksonville and Duval County, had issued a judicial decree, declaring sit-in demonstrations a dangerous activity. If you participated in a sit-in demonstration at age sixteen or younger, according to Judge Gooding, the police would arrest you as a participant in a dangerous activity. Police would also arrest the adult responsible for your demonstrating, charging that adult with "contributing to the delinquency of a minor."

The banner headline of the December 10, 1960 edition of the *Florida Star* blared, "Judge Orders Arrest of Jax Sit-In Leader."

Judge Gooding declared sit-in demonstrations to be violent and dangerous, yet no member of the Jacksonville Youth Council NAACP ever lifted a hand to harm anyone during the sit-ins. If sit-in demonstrations were dangerous, they were dangerous not because of what we did. They were dangerous because of what others did to us.

These same detectives had come to the college earlier that day with a warrant for my arrest. However, that arrest warrant read "Rodney Hurst, age 20, place of residence, New York City."

That the police thought I hailed from New York made some sense. As far as some Southern whites were concerned, "race agitators" came from the North to "indoctrinate our good colored citizens."

President Stewart explained to the detectives that I attended Edward Waters College, but lived in Jacksonville, not New York, and my age was sixteen, not twenty.

They left and returned later that day. This time the warrant read, "Rodney Hurst, age sixteen, place of residence Jacksonville, Florida." Before the detectives escorted me to the juvenile shelter, President Stewart placed a call to my mother and explained the circumstances.

My mother called Earl Johnson. Earl was not in his office, but she talked with Earl's law partner, Leander Shaw. My mother and Mr. Shaw met me at the juvenile facility.

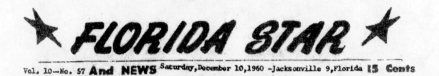

FLORIDA STAR

Vol. 10—No. 57 And NEWS Saturday,December 10,1960 –Jacksonville 9,Florida 15 Cents

Judge Orders Arrest Of Jax Sit-In Leader

Youth Leader's Arrest Seen As Move To Kill Sits-Ins

Rodney Hurst, 16, president of the Jacksonville NAACP Youth Council was arrested and charged with delinquency Thursday afternoon. Hurst will face trial Monday at 9:30 a.m. in Juvenile Judge Marion Gooding's court.

In fact, they got there before the detectives and I did. Mr. Shaw, upset that it took them "too long" to get me to the Juvenile Shelter, minced no words in showing his anger. He later said to me that the "rubber hose" did come to mind. We later laughed. It was serious though at that time.

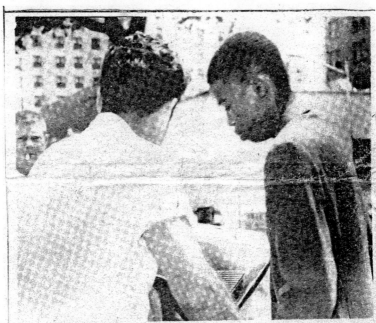

GET ON BOARD--One of the young lunch counter demonstrators is seen being taken to the juvenile shelter by law officers on orders from Juvenile Court Judge Marion Gooding.

After charging me with "contributing to the delinquency of a minor," court officials released me to the recognizance of my mother and Mr. Shaw. A hearing date was set for the following Monday, December 12, 1960.

Jacksonville police had earlier arrested Robert Ingram, a thirteen-year-old Black male. At six feet tall, Bob looked much older and mature than thirteen. Mr. Pearson would learn later from Officer Edward Hickson and other Black police officers that while in custody, Jacksonville Police Department detectives plied Bob with hamburgers and milkshakes during several "interview sessions." They repeatedly suggested to Bob that I had gotten him to demonstrate. During those days of police intimidation, it certainly would be easy for them to intimidate a thirteen year old, even one big for his age.

On the day of my hearing, civil rights supporters, members of the community, and the press packed the courtroom. Because of the size of the crowd, and the limited seating in the Juvenile courtroom, court officials allowed persons to stand. I sat in the front row with my mother, Mr. Shaw, and Mr. Johnson.

Sit-in Leader Released to His Parents

By GEORGE HARMON
Journal Staff Writer

Rodney Hurst, NAACP Youth Council leader arrested yesterday as an adult on a charge of contributing to the delinquency of a minor, was free in the custody of his parents today after it was determined he actually is a juvenile.

Police had received information that the Negro boy was between 16 and 20 years old, but a check at the Bureau of Vital Statistics resolved the issue. Hurst's birth certificate showed he was 16.

Juvenile Court Judge Marion Gooding issued a warrant yesterday charging Hurst with contributing to the delinquency of a minor by encouraging another 16-year-old Negro to participate in sit-in demonstrations at four lunch counters here Wednesday.

Warrants containing specific charges are issued only to adults. A person charged in a warrant can be tried in Criminal Court before a jury.

A juvenile is arrested on the basis of a petition which makes a general charge that the defendant is a juvenile delinquent. Such cases are handled entirely by the Juvenile Court judge.

Deputy Sheriff Robert Stringer found Hurst at Edward Waters College, where Hurst is a freshman.

Chief Probation Officer Joseph Lorimier of Juvenile Court said Stringer also checked college records, which showed that Hurst was 16. Stringer asked Hurst to accompany him to court.

After the vital statistics check resolved the question of Hurst's age, he was released in custody of his parents and ordered to appear before Judge Gooding Monday at 9:30 a.m.

Reverend Charles White McGehee attended, standing on his crutches at the rear of the courtroom. A number of NAACP members, religious leaders, and community activists attended, including Junious Bowman, executive director of the Jacksonville Urban League; Eric Simpson, editor and publisher of the *Florida Star*; Mrs. Janet Johnson, Earl's wife; my pastor, Father T. Vincent Harris of St. Philip's Episcopal Church; Reverend J. T. McMillan, pastor of Grant Memorial AME Church; Reverend J. S. Johnson of St. Stephens AME Church; Mrs. Elma Reid

Minor, an EWC faculty member, and some of her students; Marjorie Meeks; Quillie Jones; Roderick Freeman; and, of course, Mr. Pearson.

With a rap of the gavel, Judge Gooding brought the courtroom to order and directed court officials to read the charges against me. Then they brought Robert Ingram into the courtroom. Judge Gooding read his judicial decree declaring sit-in demonstrations a dangerous activity. He proceeded to take Bob's formal hearing testimony.

As this juvenile court hearing, as opposed to a trial, the judge asked the questions and directed the testimony. Judge Gooding would frequently interrupt Bob's testimony and ask, "And who told you to demonstrate?"

"Rodney Hurst," Bob answered.

Other times the judge would ask, "Rodney Hurst told you to demonstrate?"

"Yes sir," Bob responded.

Then, very dramatically, Judge Gooding asked Bob, "Now, young man, for the record and for the court, point to Rodney Hurst." I think the *Jacksonville Chronicle* called it the "moving finger." As Bob looked around the courtroom, he started moving his finger to locate and identify me. People in the courtroom started ducking as Bob moved his finger toward them.

In fact, Bob Ingram did not know me at all, and I did not know him. He certainly could not identify me as the person who asked him to demonstrate. I saw Bob for the first time that morning. Bob eventually pointed to Roderick Freeman, a Youth Council member sitting in the rear of the court. Roderick did not ask Bob to demonstrate.

Shouts of "I knew it" and "I told you so" immediately came from the gallery. Police and others involved in this thinly veiled set-up were so sure Bob knew me and could identify me, they never bothered to point me out to Bob. Judge Gooding apparently felt that Bob Ingram's identification of me in the courtroom would be a mere formality. Then my "contributing to" the so-called "delinquency of" Robert "Bob" Ingram would be a fait d'accompli. When Bob could not identify me, Mr. Johnson sprang to his feet and, in the eloquence God reserved for him, commanded the Juvenile courtroom floor and the courtroom. He spoke not only to the circumstances of the hearing, but the unconstitutional nature of the Judge's order and its violation of the United States Constitution's First Amendment right guaranteeing lawful assembly. You really liked having Earl Johnson on your side.

"Lawyer Johnson," Judge Gooding snapped, "I am not going to give you an opportunity to make a forum out of my court. Case dismissed!" After making his pronouncement, Judge Gooding got up and left the courtroom. He offered me no apology.

Only Mr. Pearson, Mr. Johnson and Mr. Shaw had considered the seriousness of the charges, and I'm not sure even they knew what they would do if Bob Ingram had somehow identified me.

Chapter 18

Mayor Haydon Burns

Nothing in all the world is more dangerous than sincere ignorance and conscientious stupidity.
- Martin Luther King

After Ax Handle Saturday, we asked Mayor Haydon Burns to appoint a Bi-Racial Committee. We felt it imperative that whites and Blacks sit and agree to agree, or sit and agree to disagree, but at least sit and establish some honest and relevant lines of communication. Mayor Burns refused. As a segregationist, he reasoned that if he appointed a biracial committee, everyone would interpret his action as condoning integration.

Mayor Haydon Burns (Courtesy Florida Photographic Collection).

Mayor Burns's reasoning, or lack thereof, represented another example of the political and social philosophy of the white establishment of the City of Jacksonville. Various newspapers throughout the State of Florida, the NAACP, the Black press, and Mr. Johnson took turns blaming Mayor Burns, and his lack of leadership, for the racial unrest in Jacksonville. They also severely criticized his decision not to appoint a biracial committee. Several out of town newspapers wrote editorials condemning the mayor's lack of action.

The national media also joined the criticism of Mayor Burns. Even the governor of the State of Florida, LeRoy Collins, had harsh words for the mayor's refusal to appoint a biracial committee. In response, Mayor Burns told Governor Collins to mind his own business.

Ministers, who were members of the white Jacksonville Ministerial Alliance, and the Black Interdenominational Ministerial Alliance asked Mayor Burns to appoint a biracial committee. Mayor Burns refused their request to discuss the city's racial problems.

Black Eye For All Florida

FOR THREE FULL DAYS now Jacksonville has been a city of tension and fear, its reputation and that of all Florida tarnished by racial violence.

The blame is not against any one individual, or even any single group. Rather it must be assessed against Negroes who sought to break down lunch counter segregation by sit-ins and picketing and then turned to less peaceful means of demonstration, the whites who sought to dissuade them by illegal means, and the officials who let the whole matter get out of hand by waiting too long to act.

As we have noted previously, lunch counter integration has come with little or no friction in those communities where it has come quietly and without fanfare through negotiation—not demonstration.

* * *

Miami Says: "It Won't Happen Here"

MIAMI -- Herald editorial staffers said that race riots such as Jacksonvia!e is experiencing "won't happen here" because:

aimed at opening lunch counters led to the violence Saturday.

Miami has had a biracial committee that has been effec-

Rodney L. Hurst Sr.

Several days after Ax Handle Saturday, Mayor Burns appeared on a local TV program and stated that Rodney Hurst and members of the NAACP Youth Council did not live in Jacksonville. He admitted he had not met any Youth Council members or their advisors, although he said he would meet with "these out-of-towners who came into our community." Burns said he especially wanted to meet with "this lawyer Johnson," who had blamed him for the riot in Jacksonville. He wanted to inform Johnson about his record as mayor—a record Johnson apparently did not know, he said.

Jax Shaken by Race Clash, Turns Into a City of Fear

By RICK TUTTLE
Herald Staff Writer

JACKSONVILLE — On a beautiful Sunday morning here a priest stood in his pulpit and spoke softly. "If Christ had walked the street of Jacksonville Saturday, He would have been horrified."

At another church a few blocks away, a minister said, "It's unbelievable that here in our town people would rise up against each other with clubs."

He said he was from Georgia. A lot of Jacksonville people are from Georgia.

"I treat them like niggers and that's what they expect. And we get along fine," he said.

At a hospital, the maintenance man patted the bulge under his shirt.

"I'm not worried," he said. He wasn't. He was obviously frightened.

"That's foolish," said another man. "Too many men get hurt with guns. They get into the wrong hands."

A late-model station wagon pulled up to the curb. A pale woman called the officer over.

"They threw rocks at us," she said. "We came off the expressway and they threw rocks at us. They are just standing in crowds on the street corners."

Mr. Johnson, in an interview with a reporter from the *Pittsburgh Courier* newspaper, blamed Mayor Burns for the riot, which, he said, had been caused by the lack of police protection downtown that Saturday. Under the City of Jacksonville's one-of-a-kind Mayor-Commission-Council form of government, law enforcement came directly under the mayor. In other words, everyone in law enforcement, including the chief of police, reported directly to the mayor.

Because Mayor Burns had expressed his desire to meet us, Mr. Pearson called the mayor's office the next day. Mayor Burns arranged a meeting in the old City Hall the following evening at 7:30 p.m.

Alton Yates, Marjorie Meeks, Henry Gardner, Mr. Pearson, Earl Johnson, and I arrived early. Mayor Burns's staff escorted us to a side entrance of Old City Hall—a security precaution, they told us. We started to leave because we felt proper protocol dictated that we walk in the front door. Then we changed our minds, figuring they would want us to leave. And it could have been a security precaution.

It was never about a hot dog and a Coke!

Gave 'Green Light' to Bigots

Jacksonville Riot Blamed on Mayor

By TREZZVANT W. ANDERSON
(Courier Roving Reporter)

JACKSONVILLE, Fla.—With this "Gateway City" of Florida back in a state of calm—for a while—a city-wide assessment of the troubles that erupted into open violence and the death of one Negro shows the most responsible sources blame Mayor Haydon Burns for what happened.

who sold the city-owned golf courses rather than integrate.

Burns is the loud segregationist.

Atty. Earl M. Johnson, counsel for most of the Negroes arrested in the rioting, placed the blame squarely upon the mayor's shoulders.

He charged the mayor with refusing to do anything whatsoever to soothe the situation, even after having been appealed to by individuals and groups. This, Attorney Johnson said, gave the green light to rabid segregationists, who felt they could do anything they pleased and get away with it.

BITTER TARGET of the Negro blasts is the Jacksonville police department, whose officers are charged with making no efforts to break up the white mob that gathered in Hemming Park early on the morning of the riots. Attorney Johnson emphasized that Negroes did not start the riots. "We were either sitting or picketing," he said.

The Courier was told that a Negro, Herbert Green, who was jailed on a charge of assault with intent to kill was a victim of police indifference.

Reportedly, a white youth drew a knife on Green in Woolworth's and Green reported it to a white policeman, saying the white boy threatened to cut him. The cop just smiled, the report said, and did nothing.

THEN THE WHITE boy came and told the officer Green had drawn a knife on him and threatened to kill him. The same officer then promptly arrested Green and charged him with assault with intent to kill. He was put under $5,000 bond.

Other instances are reported of white policemen standing by as whites attacked Negroes, and doing nothing about it.

Attorney Johnson says he is searching to see if there is any statute under which action can be taken against the local police department.

Many Negroes were arrested along with whites. Attorney Johnson said that in some cases they paid fines and were released. In other cases which were appealable, appeals were noted. As sporadic arrests continued during the week there was no specific figure as to how many Negroes had been arrested and tried.

THE NAACP, however, was handling the case of Richard Parker, a white Florida State University student and NAACP member, who was arrested and

ATTY E. M. JOHNSON
... defends Negroes

drew the heaviest sentence of any person.

He also suffered a broken jaw in an attack upon him by a white jail inmate. Mr. Johnson said Parker was jailed because he was demonstrating and not because of vagrancy, with which he was charged. Thus discrimination was clearly shown, the attorney said.

Bright, young Rodney Hurst, 16-year-old president of the NAACP Youth Council, who has Marshaled strategy for the demonstrations here, was equally as frank in laying the blame on the Mayor. "All this could have been avoided had it not been for the stand taken by our Mayor," Hurst said.

HURST POINTED OUT that Mayor Burns had repeatedly refused to show any change in his adamant position to not do anything about the protests, even though he had been importuned by the white merchants who were willing to desegregate their lunch counters if the Mayor would give his sanction.

This, Burns has refused to do, publicly saying so. He also refused to appoint a bi-racial committee to try to solve the knotty problem.

THE YOUTH COUNCIL—which has 450 members—decided to postpone its demonstrations after the riots, "not because of fear of any bodily harm," but to give time to responsible white and Negro citizens to get together to try to work things out.

POLICE CHIEF Luther Reynolds told the students they would be arrested if they didn't leave the store. They left and went into a huddle in the council.

It was decided then to do a thorough planning and research job to find out what the score was with the downtown stores. The youths amassed statistical data and the amount of Negro patronage of each store, the value in money, the employment pattern of the stores, etc.

Finally, after about two months, Alton Yates, chairman of the program and research committee, presented the matter to the executive board, and three weeks ago the council was ready to start.

The research job was so thorough that the council knew that Cohen's had at least 500 accounts from the 894 Negro teachers in Duval County. Hurst was at one time a bus boy in the restaurant of Cohen's and had talked "better jobs" with the manager there.

THE YOUTHS were ready to attack and they did. The local dailies put a "news blackout" on their activities and kept it on until the picture erupted into violence that Saturday. During the picketing and sitting, the stores have suffered a loss of Negro business, a loss they feel keenly.

They want to accede to the Negro youths, but want official city sanction, to guard against white reprisal acts.

That is where Mayor Burns, an ardent segregationist, who is still bitter because Negro Jaxons voted against him in his bid for Governor last May, won't cooperate.

MRS. HURLEY, on Wednesday sent a letter to the Justice Department asking it to intervene because of the obvious refusal or inability of the Jacksonville police department to protect Negro citizens as demonstrated during the riots and for other reasons.

She said the mass meetings on Sundays will be continued.

The first one at St. Paul AME Church was a big success, with over 1,400 citizens turning out and pledging their support to the movement.

We finally reasoned that if we left, the mayor could publicly say that the Youth Council NAACP wanted only to criticize him and not meet with him. We stayed.

Mayor Burns met us in the main conference room in Old City Hall. We sat around a large table. Mr. Johnson and two other Black males, whom we did not recognize, sat in chairs behind us.

There were several unidentified whites whom we pegged as police or part of the Mayor's security team. Mayor Burns opened the meeting with several condescending comments about his good race relations with his "Negro citizens," and his assertion that the "race riot instigators were all from out of town."

Though the mayor never asked us where we lived, we told him that all of us were from Jacksonville and lived in Jacksonville. I asked the mayor why no police officers had patrolled the downtown area on Ax Handle Saturday. Expecting the question, he read his response from a piece of paper, justifying all police assignments downtown that day with the exception of four police officers. He never identified the four or their assignments.

Before we could ask, one of the unidentified Blacks in the room, whom we figured were members of the mayor's staff, raised his hand to ask the mayor a question. "Since you accounted for the whereabouts of everyone except those four policemen, why couldn't they have been assigned to provide protection for those children downtown?"

We looked at each other—the question caught everyone off guard. We did not expect someone in the room other than us to challenge the Mayor. Obviously upset that this man had asked the question, he referred to both men by name, and then had Security escort them from the meeting. He tried to move on, but Alton Yates again asked about the assignment of the four officers. He never gave us a sufficient answer.

Most observers considered Mayor Burns a well-informed politician. His friends and those who knew him well called him "Slick." Yet he made a critically strategic mistake during the meeting. He referred to attorney Earl Johnson several times as "that Lawyer Johnson," whom he criticized for blaming the mayor for the riot. The mayor had obviously paid little attention to our earlier introductions, because Mr. Johnson sat directly behind us. We did not let on that Mr. Johnson was present. Expecting later fireworks, we were not disappointed.

Finally, Mr. Johnson raised his hand. When the mayor recognized him, Earl began by saying he was that "lawyer Johnson" to whom the Mayor kept referring.

From the moment Mr. Johnson started to speak, until he concluded his explanation of the issues, he did not back off blaming the mayor for the riot. We loved listening to him—he was mesmerizing and intellectually informed. As Earl Johnson continued his comments, the room just got quiet. In the Black community, when you really want to illustrate what quiet is, you say, "it was so quiet, you could hear a rat piss on cotton." That is how quiet the room got after Mr. Johnson's first few comments. Although obviously respectful, Mr. Johnson spoke several minutes, making point after point and continuing to lay responsibility for the riot at the feet of the Mayor.

When he finished, for all intents and purposes, the meeting was over. Mr. Johnson left nothing for anyone else to say. We had not met with the mayor with any goal in mind. Mayor Burns had wanted to meet us, and we wanted to meet him. Irrespective of the results, we communicated, which is more than he would allow by not appointing a biracial committee. We courteously thanked the mayor and he thanked us, and never met with him again.

VOL XVI NO. 51   JACKSONVILLE, FLORIDA, FRIDAY, SEPTEMBER 16, 1960   10 CENTS

Negro Paper Blames Burns

A streamer on copies of the Pittsburgh Courier, nationally circulated negro weekly, reaching Jacksonville, read: "BLAME JAX RACE RIOT ON MAYOR."

Seven riot yarns were in the issue. A feature told the history of Rodney Hurst, 16, negro, president of the NAACP Youth Council. It said he decided to organize the recent sit-ins, while working as a bus boy in the Cohen's restaurant, observing the menial jobs assigned to negroes. It said the council has 450 members.

Its story on Burns said in part:

"Most responsible sources blame Mayor Haydon Burns for what happened ... (he) is loud segregationist ... Atty. Mark M. Johnson, counsel for most of the negroes arrested, placed the blame squarely on the mayor's shoulders ... charged the mayor refused to do anything ... gave the green light to rabid segregationists."

Rodney L. Hurst Sr.

In the meantime, the *Florida Star* and other newspapers continued to publish articles about Mayor Burns and the city's political structure. The paper said they merely stood by while others in the community worked to try to bridge an apparently widening racial divide. Of course, the Jacksonville Chronicle also wrote about the riot by quoting Black newspapers in real Chronicle-style.

Jacksonville's political representatives and the *Jacksonville Chronicle* continued to call Youth Council members Communists and worse. In the meantime, an editorial appeared in the *Tampa Tribune* under the headline, "Jacksonville Story . . . No. 2":

"For some months before he ran for Governor last spring, Mayor Haydon Burns traveled the state giving a film talk entitled "The Jacksonville Story." It was an account of the impressive progress in downtown redevelopment made during his administration.

For the last week, the nation's press has been headlining another "Jacksonville story." This one is much less flattering; it depicts a city shaken by the worst racial conflict the South has seen this year.

Mayor Burns says the press reports exaggerated the trouble here. Perhaps so, but the fact that 85 persons were sentenced in Municipal Court on charges growing out of the disorders shows the situation was bad enough. Jacksonville's difficulties remind us that behind a city's towering expressways, its shiny new skyscrapers and its booming businesses may lie the combustible elements of disaster.

"We cannot say whether ...poor housing and very limited recreational facilities... are worse in Jacksonville than in Tampa or Miami. But, in one important respect, Jacksonville apparently was worse off than other major Florida cities. That was in the area of cooperation between the races."

As long as men of reason and good will can sit down together, there is no racial problem which can't be defused before it bursts into violence.

The latest "Jacksonville story" tell us that preventives are infinitely better . . . and cheaper . . . than repairs."

From the perspective of a fellow Florida city, Jacksonville had a long way to go.

The Mayor, however, seemed not to realize this. He would later run for governor of the State of Florida and win. When he ran for re-election, with many members of the sit-in generation now of voting age, he lost.

Chapter 19

The Jacksonville Chronicle

You can't separate peace from freedom because no one can be at peace unless he has his freedom.
- Malcolm X

In Jacksonville during the late fifties and early sixties, the *Jacksonville Chronicle* not only espoused the segregationist point of view, Blacks in Jacksonville considered the *Chronicle* the media outlet for both the Ku Klux Klan and the White Citizens Council.

We did not consider reportorial objectivity to be one of the strong suits of publisher Sam Melson, yet occasionally he would come through with some interesting jewels. In the *Chronicle*'s August 26, 1960 edition, the paper referred to sit-in demonstrations at Cohen Brothers Department Store:

"Later that day, there was no news of the events [sit-ins] even on Channel 4, which carries a short daily news program for Cohen's and which apparently submitted to its wishes for no publicity. Some news outlets claim the best way to hamper the sit-ins is to ignore them-just like one would ignore a small fire."

According to the *Chronicle*, its regular contributors, and its readers, sit-in demonstrators were Communists or Communist-inspired.

An advertisement appeared in the September 2, 1960 issue of the *Jacksonville Chronicle* that practically jumped off the page. Vicious and hate-centered, it was the kind of fare that epitomized the paper's viewpoint. It read (in part):

WE SALUTE YOU

We hereby pay our respects and gratitude to the following stores who have so courageously resisted the recent Communist Inspired lunch counter "sit-in" demonstration attempts here in Jacksonville:

**McCRORYS KRESS GRANT'S
SEARS-ROEBUCK COHEN BROTHERS**

MORRISON'S CAFETERIA WOOLWORTH'S

After the above headline, the first line of the ad read:

"In public recognition of your intrepid refusal to serve Negroes at the WHITE lunch counters in your stores, we go on record as heartily urging the WHITE citizens of Duval County to increase their patronage of your WHITE American stores. Thus far you have done a great job helping us maintain segregation in this section of the state."

Quoting excerpts from the ad:

ATTENTION ALL WHITE CITIZENS OF JACKSONVILLE AND DUVAL COUNTY!

President Lincoln was an ardent Segregationist. The greatest Segregationist of all is God Almighty. He divided the nations and separated the races. That spells RACIAL SEGREGATION!

The one-quarter page ad went on to say that the Bible not only teaches a message of racial segregation, but also strongly condemns racial integration.

In addition to calling the NAACP "Communist-inspired," the ad typified the hate-filled language directed at Blacks who had the courage of their convictions to try to exercise their rights as Americans.

Interestingly, publisher Melson inserted a disclaimer in the ad: "Eight lines of the originally submitted copy, appearing here, were deleted on grounds that the text could contribute to racial tensions." Could they have written something too strong for Sam Melson?

Other parts of the ad were as inflammatory, but the last line helps you get the picture: "We are going to defend Christ, America, and the White Race." The White American Christian Patriots of Duval County paid for the ad.

In the same September 2, 1960 *Jacksonville Chronicle* edition, in large bold headlines, Sam Melson blamed Florida Governor LeRoy Collins for the riots of Ax Handle Saturday, while also blaming Jacksonville Mayor Haydon Burns, but for different reasons.

He accused Governor Collins, considered a racial moderate, for supporting the "rights of Blacks to demonstrate at lunch counters," and he blamed Burns for not having the police arrest the demonstrators.

Rodney L. Hurst Sr.

FRIDAY, SEPTEMBER 2, 1960   10 CENTS

BLAME BURNS-COLLINS FOR RACE RIOTS

Gov. Leroy Collins who publicly advocated sit-ins by negroes at white lunch counters and Mayor Haydon Burns, whose weak police policy against unlawful insistence of the negroes that they be served were drawing principal blame this week for the current racial riots here. Local papers called them 'racial unrest'. Outside papers called it "race riots". The daily Jax newspapers and tv news programs also were not held blameless for their wholesale suppression of two weeks of incidents which preceded the major racial eruptions of last Saturday-Sunday. It was front page news in all newspapers of the nation except the Times-Union.

Two dead was the toll at the first of this week with part of this news also kept from the public--in local papers--because police said the pistol death of one negro shot down by white

JACKSONVILLE, FLORIDA FRIDAY, OCTOBER 7, 1960

Rev. Kissling On Race Mixing Board

A group which Mrs. Eleanor Roosevelt says "is working for integration in the South" has just issued an appeal for money in a pamphlet adver-

142

NAACP Negro Woman Bosses Race Doings

Apparently, Ruby Hurley, Atlanta negro woman, who is regional director for the National Association for Advancement of the Colored People can turn the faucet off and on--as she wishes--on racial unrest creating incidents in Jacksonville.

In the role of her press agents, a channel 12 tv announcer and also Herb Kaslow, the NBC Jew sent into Jacksonville to stress the pinko side of the recent race riots, in conformity with the race mixing stand of the Jewish owners of NBC and the Jewish owners of both Jax tv outlets, sponsored appearance of the Hurley woman on tv 12 or both local and national broadcasts.

The NAACP director said he felt the situation was well in hand prior to last weekend, that she had told the outh council of the organization not to try any more sits at white lunch counters, reate trouble at the Saturday ro football game nor wade-ins t local beaches on Labor ey.

The "violence" end of the tuation brought on by the AACP sponsored sit-ins re blamed by the woman on 'ive local negro gangs, mbering 2,000 to 3,000." it, she assured that they would behave--for a time. The woman over the week i announced that the "negro npaign to end segregation Jacksonville would con-ue."

"This is Ruby."

In a later series of editorials, Sam Melson labeled white ministers as "race-mixing preachers" and he singled out Reverend Albert Kissling as one of the ministers leading the integration movement.

The Chronicle even referred to the National Council of Churches as a Communist-blighted organization that "fell in line with the Synagogue of Satan." The job of purging "race-mixing preachers" from

Jacksonville's midst belonged to the *Chronicle*'s readers. (We could only imagine the message that sent.)

An article that appeared in the September 9, 1960 edition under the headline "NAACP Negro Woman Bosses Race Doings" also typified the *Chronicle*.

An excerpt from that article (as published):

"Apparently Ruby Hurley, Atlanta negro woman, who is Regional Director of the NAACP, can turn the faucet off and on . . . as she wishes . . . on racial unrest creating incidents in Jacksonville. [Melson always spelled Negro with a small "n".]

"In the role of her press agents, a Channel 12 tv announcer and also Herb Kaplow, the NBC Jew sent into Jacksonville to stress the pinko side of the recent race riots, in conformity with the race mixing stand of the Jewish owners of NBC and the Jewish owners of both Jax tv outlets, sponsored [an] appearance of the Hurley woman on tv 12 for both local and national broadcasts."

A picture of Mrs. Hurley followed the article with the caption, "This is Ruby." Melson never referred to Mrs. Hurley as Mrs. He always called her Ruby or Hurley or that "negro woman."

Chapter 20

State Representative George Stallings

Black people have always been in America's wilderness in search of a promised land.
                                                            - Dr. Cornel West

Reverend Robert Gisler, pastor of the Snyder Memorial Methodist Church, asked Jacksonville State Representative George B. Stallings Jr. to serve on a biracial committee. Representative Stallings refused, citing as his principal reason his opposition to racial integration as advocated by the preachers. Under the headline "Raps Preachers On Integration," the *Jacksonville Chronicle* published Representative Stallings's full refusal letter on page 4 in its Friday, September 2, 1960 edition.

State Representative George Stallings (Courtesy Florida Photographic Collection).

"This letter is in answer to your invitation by telephone yesterday asking me to participate on a committee of local citizens, called for the special purpose of appointing a bi-racial committee to allegedly solve the tense racial situation that has developed in Jacksonville. First, I must refuse to accept the invitation."

The letter continued, "To preface my reasons for refusing, I will point out several basic and well-known truths which have been held for years by the responsible citizens of the South, namely that integration of the white and colored races in any area of community life stimulates strife and thus mitigates against the peace and good order of the community; that integration destructively affects the safety, health, morals, peace, and general welfare of the community and that is should be resisted to the full extent of the law."

Stallings went on to say, "Jacksonville now has a serious problem of racial tension. To solve the problem, one must first seek the cause of it and then proceed to apply the remedy to the root of the matter. The cause of our particular problem is the attempt on the part of Communist inspired organizations (headed by NAACP and CORE) to force integration upon the people of the South in all areas of community life. Many of these organizations are headed by Communist-fronters. At present they are using 'sit-in' demonstrations to achieve their goal. By the use of semantics, such demonstrations are falsely labeled peaceful and non-violent. In reality they are flagrant and wanton examples of trespass upon the rights of private property.

"The recent racial strife in Jacksonville is an evil that has its origin in the race mixing organizations of the Negro Race. The sit-in demonstrations are calculated efforts to force integration upon the community by means of lawless acts masquerading under false labels of respectability.

"In the face of such well known facts, the Ministerial Alliance favors the appointment of a bi-racial committee to formulate a solution to the problem. The leader of the NAACP Youth Council among others has been invited to serve on the committee which has been called to appoint the bi-racial committee. Under the circumstances, there is no justification for the appointment of a bi-racial committee. To place members of the Negro Race (who for the most part, are NAACP leaders) on a committee of this sort is nothing short of an endorsement and recognition of the very organization that is the root and branch of the evil that the committee would be attempting to cure.

"In Florida, any bi-racial committee is doomed to failure from the outset. It is completely inconsistent to attempt to solve an unjustifiable, illegal situation by the creation of a bi-racial committee whose actions would be to condone the illegality of the sit-ins and to cloak such demonstrations with the garments of respectability.

"The Jacksonville situation has resulted from the initial breaking of law by members of Negro race-mixing organizations. The solution to lawlessness is the strict enforcement of the broken law. It cannot be solved by the formation of bi-racial committees to justify the breaking of such laws using false premises and dogmas as a basis. Too many ministers are promoting integration on the false assumption that it is a moral issue. The problem confronting Jacksonville today is one that is strictly legal. The solution lies in the strict enforcement of law and in loyal adherence to the established principles of constitutional government.

"The Legislature has done its duty by enacting laws to give protection to the owners of private property from unlawful trespass and encroachments upon it. It is the duty of local merchants and citizens to invoke the existing trespass laws of Florida against all violators. Any surrender on their part to the insidious demands of the race-mixers will only inflame an already bad situation and give rise to increased violence in the community."

The Honorable State Representative George Stallings Jr. concluded, "For the above reasons, I deplore the appointment of a bi-racial committee and decline the invitation to serve on the committee which will appoint it."

If you wanted a social and political commentary that represented Jacksonville's white political establishment during the late fifties and early sixties, the Honorable George Stallings Jr., as a member of the Florida House of Representatives, just gave it to you.

Chapter 21

Telling the Ax Handle Saturday Story

*"Players in this drama of frustration and indignity are
not commas or semicolons in a legislative thesis; they
are people, human beings, and citizens of the United
States of America."*

—Roy Wilkins

After Ax Handle Saturday and the national publicity about Jacksonville,
the NAACP asked that I travel to several cities in the South to tell the
"Jacksonville story." They called it a mini-speaking tour. However, as
a student at Edward Waters College, I could only travel on weekends,
though I could leave occasionally on a Thursday. Edward Waters had a
great and understanding faculty, but I still had to complete my college
assignments.

I attended my first major civil rights conference at Frogmore, South
Carolina in the St. Helena Islands in September 1960 when invited to
speak about Ax Handle Saturday and the Jacksonville story. Several
civil rights organizations that actively participated in the civil rights
movement would send a number of representatives. The civil rights
movement embraced several different philosophies, and we needed to
get together from time to time to discuss them.

Penn Center, originally called Penn Normal School, was established
in 1862—about six months before the Emancipation Proclamation, and
about three years before the Civil War ended. It was to be the venue.

Penn Center is one of approximately thirty schools built on St
Helena's Island as part of the Port Royal Experiment. Its leaders
were philanthropists, abolitionists, and Quaker missionaries from
Pennsylvania. They came to the Beaufort area after Union soldiers
took control of the Port Royal Sound, forcing the Confederates to flee.
Their purpose was to help black Sea Islanders prepare for freedom by

teaching them how to read and survive economically. They named the school in honor of their home state and Quaker activist William Penn. (Penn Center web site)

I left Jacksonville Thursday afternoon aboard a Greyhound bus en route to Beaufort, South Carolina and the St. Helena Islands. Conference staff and Jacksonville Youth Council NAACP members who drove were to meet me at Beaufort's Greyhound Bus Station. I asked the bus driver to let me know when the bus got to Beaufort. Maybe he forgot. Maybe he knew one of the several drivers whom my grandmother had once embarrassed when we traveled to Aiken. Maybe I was asleep when he announced Beaufort—I sat at the back of the bus. Maybe he figured I should know my destination. Maybe he knew me and wanted me to miss the conference. Bottom line, I missed my stop.

When I awoke, the driver announced Charleston, South Carolina. *Charleston, South Carolina?* How close was Charleston to Beaufort? Not close enough, I would find out. So now I had to get to Beaufort. There were no cell phones then, and, in any event, I did not have a telephone number to call. Everyone expected me before 9 p.m. It was now after close to 11 p. m.

The bus driver did arrange for me to board a bus heading in Beaufort's direction. However, because the return trip did not have a scheduled stop in Beaufort, the bus driver had to put me off on the highway somewhere outside of Beaufort. He did so after 1 a.m.

So here I am, the president of the Jacksonville Youth Council NAACP, stranded somewhere in South Carolina, on my way to a civil rights conference at that bastion of racial agitation in Frogmore, South Carolina—Penn Center—and without my luggage. I guessed they had removed it from the bus when it stopped in Beaufort. (I did not need luggage at that moment.)

I am now standing in front of a closed gas station with the globed fuel pumps—the abandoned ones you usually see while traveling the South. There were no pay telephones. I did not know my location. On the other hand, did the wrong persons know my location? You cannot imagine how many things crossed my mind at the time.

I went into stealth mode. I heard every cricket and wild animal in the world. You name them; I heard them. One cannot imagine what goes through one's mind when stranded in the middle of nowhere. Even if I were inclined to steal a car, which I was not, I could not drive, so that consideration certainly did not make the possibility list.

As car lights approached from the highway, I hid at the side of a building, and started mapping my strategy of what to do if I had to be there for a while. How could I know that "search teams" were looking for me? After dodging and hiding from cars for what must have been more than two hours, a Black cab driver, one of the "search teams" looking for me, finally spotted me at the side of the building. He called out my name. I did not answer. He drove around to the side of the building and got out of his cab, shining a flashlight. He called my name again. I answered. He told me he had been looking for me for more than three hours, and had visited that same location several times because it was a bus drop-off point. I told him I didn't know teams were looking for me. Besides, I was scared. I asked him what time it was. It was after 3 a.m. He laughed. I failed to see the humor.

Much to the relief of the conference hosts, I finally made it to the Penn Center. Mr. Pearson and a number of the conference attendees were still awake. Mr. Pearson had alerted conference staff, who knew I was overdue.

Notwithstanding my foray into the hinterlands of South Carolina, I could feel the excitement at the Penn Center. The conference lasted three days and featured a full line-up—a veritable who's who of the civil rights movement—except they were not who's who yet. Most of the attendees came from SNCC, NAACP college chapters, and Dr. Martin Luther King's relatively new Southern Christian Leadership Conference. I represented the only NAACP youth council. Some of the speakers, discussion group leaders, and attendees would later make their impact on the Movement, people like Dr. Martin Luther King Jr., Reverend Jesse Jackson, Stokeley Carmichael, H. Rap Brown, John Lewis, Charles McDew, Diane Nash, James Bevel, Marion Barry, James Foreman, and Julian Bond, to name just a few. I spoke during one of the main sessions. Jacksonville, Florida and Ax Handle Saturday still commanded a lot of attention, and I considered this conference a major think-tank strategy session of the Movement during 1960.

In October of 1960, I traveled to Richmond, Virginia, to speak to the annual meeting of the Virginia State Conference of NAACP Branches. With one of the largest memberships in the nation, the Virginia State

Conference of NAACP Branches had a roster large enough to have a paid executive secretary (Lester Banks). I stayed with his family during my visit to Richmond.

I spoke to several conference workshop sessions at Virginia Union University, a Historically Black University in Richmond. A number of attendees were already familiar with the Jacksonville story and Ax Handle Saturday—the Jacksonville Youth Council NAACP had made its mark in the country. Though the fully orchestrated "news blackout" by the Jacksonville press eliminated the most obvious source of news, the national press, the NAACP press office, and the Black press did an excellent job reporting nationally what had happened in Jacksonville.

I gave the conference attendees the full Jacksonville story, including the Ax Handle Saturday story. Just about every major city in the South, and especially cities where there was a Historically Black College and University, had experienced sit-in demonstrations. The Virginia Conference represented another opportunity to share those experiences. Of course, Virginia Union and Richmond, Virginia had their own unfortunate experiences, with police arresting demonstrators for trespassing and using police dogs to intimidate demonstrators.

On Sunday, the last day of the conference, the Virginia State NAACP Conference of Branches held its annual mass meeting at the Richmond Mosque (now known as the Richmond Landmark Theater).

The Mosque was an imposing yet beautiful building. It was lavish and luxurious when built. Construction on the Mosque started in February 1926, and took two years to finish. Formally opened on October 28, 1927 by ACCA Temple of the Mystic Shrine, the building has an exotic splendor. Into the dome alone went 75,000 square feet of gold leaf, and another 35,000 square feet of aluminum leaf. The Auditorium decorations included Saracenic decorations and five paintings bordering the proscenium arch of the stage. Ornamental tile used in the interior came from Spain, Italy, and Tunis, as did lush carpets, silken curtains, and paintings, all of which suggested the rich tents and equipment of a Saracenic nobleman. The auditorium sits nearly 5,000. The City of Richmond bought the building May 16, 1940. (*Richmond Landmark Theater homepage*)

We looked forward to hearing Roy Wilkins, the executive secretary of the NAACP. Whether or not you were an NAACP member, you always wanted to hear Mr. Wilkins. With NAACP youth councils and college chapters in the middle of sit-in demonstrations, boycotts, and the picketing of businesses throughout the South, Wilkins personified Black power, and brought an authentic message about the status of the movement in the country.

The meeting began with the expected pomp and ceremony as dignitaries and other invited guests paraded onto the stage. Virginia NAACP members, supporters, and friends of the NAACP packed the Mosque. As a platform guest, I excitedly took part in the procession. I tried to look for my group from Jacksonville—they had made the trip in Mr. Pearson's station wagon—but I did not see them.

Mr. Banks introduced Mr. Wilkins, who came to the podium amid a standing ovation and thunderous applause. Mr. Wilkins then said something that really caught my attention. He said that, even though the program listed him as the speaker, he knew that everyone would want to hear from "young Rodney Hurst, the sixteen-year-old president of the Jacksonville Youth Council NAACP," who would tell everyone the story of Ax Handle Saturday in Jacksonville, Florida. He then said, "Rodney come here and tell Virginia the Jacksonville story." Had Roy Wilkins just invited me to speak to 4000-plus people in the Richmond Mosque? Yes, he had.

As I anxiously made my way to the podium, I looked for Mr. Pearson and my Jacksonville group. I remembered his constant advice—when speaking in public, relax, be comfortable at the podium, and never lock your knees. I also remembered him saying that most people get nervous when speaking because they do not know what to say. I had a quick flashback to my junior high days, when he gave me public speaking seminars as I rode in his car.

I had spoken about Ax Handle Saturday on a number of occasions. I knew what to say, but I still could not find Mr. Pearson and the members of the Jacksonville Youth Council. After I thanked Mr. Wilkins and my hosts, Mr. and Mrs. Banks, and acknowledged the platform guests, and the officials of the Virginia State Conference of Branches NAACP, a light went on. Just ask Mr. Pearson and the members of the Jacksonville Youth Council NAACP to stand. There they were, sitting on the first row. Whew! I felt more comfortable.

Telling the Ax Handle story made my adrenaline flow. The more applause I received, the more I became passionate about our mission in Jacksonville. Of course, the climate of the country and the climate of the civil rights movement made this a very receptive audience. I wanted to make this audience, some 800 miles from Jacksonville, understand that we did not sit in to eat a hot dog and drink a Coke. At issue was human dignity and respect, I said. Our resolve, I added, was to "become a part of the solution and not a part of the problem." We all needed "to understand that freedom was not free." The various messages resonated quite well. I guess I spoke maybe 15 or 20 minutes. Then Mr. Wilkins came back to the podium again and delivered his update of the country. He acknowledged the Jacksonville Youth Council and Mr. Pearson again, and gave a state-by-state update of NAACP activities. It was riveting.

* * *

I spoke at Johnson C. Smith University, an HBCU in Charlotte, North Carolina, in November of 1960. The College Chapter of the NAACP at Johnson C. Smith invited us. This time, we drove. Mr. Pearson again drove his station wagon, and Alton Yates drove his car. We had guest dormitory accommodations at Johnson C. Smith. They were not ready when we arrived, so Mr. Pearson, a member of the Alpha Phi Alpha fraternity, arranged for us to stay in their frat house until our rooms were ready. He did something with his hands and said something to one of his frat brothers, who he later identified as the head of the Alphas. I asked him what he said to his brother, and he called it a "distress call." We were impressed. Once again, the Jacksonville story was front and center.

Traveling to conferences and to college campuses to talk about the Jacksonville story and Ax Handle Saturday became an experience in itself. It was like traveling to a family reunion. Every community and campus where I spoke could easily identify with the Jacksonville story, and the fact that Black youth were taking a stand. Our crowds were always engaging and receptive.

My next trip took me to Savannah, Georgia, to address the Georgia State Conference of Branches NAACP. W. W. Law, the state president, and a civil rights icon, had invited us. His main job involved working as a mail carrier for the Post Office.

W. W. Law, a crusader for justice and the civil rights of Blacks, served as president of the Savannah National Association for the Advancement of Colored People (NAACP) chapter from 1950 to 1976, and came to be known in Georgia as "Mr. Civil Rights." Law retired as Savannah NAACP president in 1976, after serving for twenty-six years. He then turned his attention to the preservation of Black history and historic buildings. He established the Savannah-Yamacraw Branch of the Association for the Study of Afro-American Life and History (ASALH). Law died on July 28, 2002, at his Savannah home.

Though Savannah was close to Jacksonville, Mr. Law still wanted us to come and give the details of our sit-in demonstrations. Blacks often could never get the real story unless they heard it directly from the story-makers. Although we were never reluctant to travel and share our story, we did have one exception. National NAACP headquarters did not want us traveling to Alabama and Mississippi. According to their intelligence, the danger level and the potential for harm were simply too high. We deferred to their judgment and though NAACP chapters in both states offered to pay our expenses to come, we turned down several requests to speak in both states. The National NAACP warnings were painfully prophetic, as history unfortunately bears out.

Georgia's State NAACP conference also had a mass meeting on the last day of its conference. Once again, I told the Jacksonville story, though I was not the featured speaker. Mass meetings were about hearing and sharing the message. They were about networking and keeping each other informed, motivated, and involved. We did have access to the Black press, which eventually became the only media that really told the story. We had no other access to the media. Most times, the sponsoring NAACP chapter or branch did not invite the media. We simply stood before a group, usually in church, and told our story. As Mr. Pearson had instructed us, we simply presented a "narration of facts, in chronological order, with their cause and effect."

Chapter 22

The Bi-Racial Committee

"It is a blessing to die for a cause, because you can so easily die for nothing."

—Andrew Young

Because of the lack of leadership shown by the mayor and others in political authority, our boycott, which we dubbed our "selective buying" program against downtown Jacksonville, proved to be quite successful. It was September. We were fast approaching the time of the year when many persons and especially Blacks would start "putting clothes and merchandise in lay-away" for Christmas. Merchandise could "remain in the store's lay-away" for 90 days. Stores depended on their Christmas sales to make that year's profit margin. Having already cut into a portion of that profit margin during the sit-ins, the resulting downtown riot took care of another portion.

Our branches received a memo from the NAACP asking that we not call the withholding of our monies from white businesses a "boycott." There would be legal challenges if we did. Instead, the NAACP directed us to call the boycott "a selective buying program." So we created a "selective buying" program for downtown Jacksonville after initially calling it a boycott. It was still successful.

Race Relations Talks Planned in City

Richard Francis Parker in Jail Again. Page 22.

By JIMMY WALKER
Journal Staff Writer

A meeting to explore ways of avoiding racial trouble was called here today in the wake of new efforts by Negroes to integrate practically every public facility in Jacksonville.

The first meeting of the community relations committee of the Jacksonville Area Chamber of Commerce was scheduled at 4 p.m. in the chamber building.

By one day it follows a suit by Negroes seeking an end to segregation practices in Duval schools. And less than a week ago, Federal District Judge Bryan Simpson announced he would issue a sweeping order banning segregation at city parks,

the zoo, the coliseum, Gator Bowl, baseball park, and the auditorium now under construction.

Alfred C. Ulmer Sr., who heads the chamber committee, said several recommendations have been given the committee.

The meeting takes place against a background of around Negro action over the state, including attempts to buy tickets to four theatres restricted to white patrons in Miami.

In Tallahassee, picketing of lunch-counter stores produced one incident yesterday. White teen-agers tore up picketers' signs but no physical violence developed.

Woolworths downtown store and May-Cohens in Jacksonville yesterday were again the scenes of attempted integration at lunch counters by young Negroes, joined by an unidentified white woman. They were ignored at the Woolworths counter and barred from the May-Cohens dining room.

The Chamber of Commerce committee was organized after

Mayor Haydon Burns declined in September to appoint a bi-racial committee. He said the lunch-counter demonstrations were a problem of the merchants.

Sit-ins were abandoned by the Youth Council of the National Association for the Advancement of Colored People in late August after a weekend flareup of violence. They began again last week.

Fourteen Negro children were named plaintiffs in the suit to end school segregation here. The suit followed the pattern of those filed earlier in Hillsborough, Palm Beach, Dade, Escambia and Volusia counties. There has been no decision from federal courts in any of them.

Negroes won a federal court order to integrate Jacksonville's two municipal golf courses and their clubhouses last year, but the city closed the courses and sold them to private operators.

Once again, the Black community had to internalize the need to sacrifice.

With the continued intransigence of the mayor and the success of the selective buying campaign against downtown businesses, the two ministerial alliances, the Jacksonville Chamber of Commerce, and the business community finally got involved with the biracial committee issue. It obviously made good community sense and good business sense.

Representatives from the Black Interdenominational Ministerial Alliance, the white Jacksonville Ministerial Alliance, representatives from the NAACP Youth Council and NAACP Adult Branch, and businessmen from the Jacksonville Chamber of Commerce started meeting weekly at Snyder Memorial Church.

Members of the committee included Fred Schultz, Reverend Robert Gisler, Reverend J. S. Johnson, Earl M. Johnson, Rev. Albert Kissling, Mr. Pearson, and me. Schultz would play a key role in the ultimate decision of the committee. The list also included other ministers, representatives of the business community, and several downtown department store managers.

At the outset, we made sure the committee members, and especially the white committee members, understood that white lunch counters were targets of sit-in demonstrations because "they were visible vestiges of segregation; and because of issues with how downtown businesses accepted our money." We further explained that sit-in demonstrations were not about eating a hot dog and a Coke, but were always about human dignity and respect. In short, we made it clear we were not meeting just about integrating lunch counters.

KING KONG KLOWN---Masked and dressed in an ape suit, an anti-sit-inner, reported to be a member of the local hate group attempts to heckle the Negro student pickets demonstrating outside Cohen's department store. Aside from the brutally reportedly accorded a Negro youth at the juvenile shelter, only minor incidents were listed.

There were other issues to consider: the lack of downtown retail sales persons for Blacks; the integration of all eating establishments, and not just the lunch counters; the need for more Black law enforcement officials; the lack of city transportation bus drivers; and the lack of Black firefighters. We placed a veritable cornucopia of issues on the table.

Those in attendance were quick to point out that those issues went beyond the scope of the committee.

I wanted to yell, "We know that." Because the committee did not carry "official" status, we knew that some of these issues would not get to first base, but we wanted to make sure they were on the table anyway.

One of the members of the Jacksonville Civil Service Board had publicly stated earlier that Blacks were afraid of heights, and because Blacks would have to climb ladders as firefighters, they could not qualify.

The meetings began slowly as communications between whites and Blacks got under way for perhaps the first time in the history of the Jacksonville community. Without the official sanction of Mayor Haydon Burns, we were meeting as the first Jacksonville Bi-Racial Committee.

Acrimony initially prevailed. There were charges and countercharges relative to attitudes and segregation, with the business community representatives complaining it was unfair to hold them responsible for the integration of lunch counters. Some of the businessmen on the committee were still upset with the sit-in demonstrations, and resented serving on the committee with Mr. Pearson and me as representatives of the NAACP Youth Council. They had a real problem but they could do nothing about it.

One member of the committee accused me of being too arrogant because I disagreed with his comments though I "respectfully disagreed." Arrogance to him meant that a teenaged Black male had disagreed with him for probably the first time in his life. Whites serving on the committee had to deal with us as equals for probably the first time in their lives. (Of course, the ministers on the committee tried to keep us as spiritually grounded as the Good Lord would allow, given the circumstances.)

After we temporarily called off the sit-ins, white members of the committee felt we should temporarily discontinue the picketing, too, while we were meeting and negotiating. They did not like the implied threat; certainly, they did not want it to appear to their community that Blacks were holding their feet to the fire, as we were. We politely and courteously told them we would continue to talk with them, but continue to picket, too.

The talks stalled. Some blamed schedules and time constraints. Others charged that Mr. Pearson and I as Youth Council representatives were negotiating in bad faith. Others claimed the meetings were useless because the committee had no official sanction. We counter-charged that the white community did not intend to negotiate in good faith, and that these excuses were a subterfuge to keep them from doing the right thing. Moreover, the right thing, in this instance, meant integrating the downtown lunch counters, at least as a start.

It became obvious that the business community did not see how serious we were about the boycott (selective buying campaign) of downtown Jacksonville stores. In our opinion, committee members were disingenuously stalling, hoping to outwait Blacks regardless of the importance of the issues, and believing that if they were patient enough, we would capitulate and go back to business as usual. Not this time, we decided.

Periodically, we updated the Youth Council and the adult branch of the NAACP on committee developments. After voting to discontinue our participation, Mr. Pearson and I left the committee. Various committee members criticized us for leaving. We did not mind the criticism. We decided it was more important to maintain the dignity of the civil rights movement than to meet just to say we were meeting. Even at age sixteen, it did not take me long to recognize a lack of intent to do the right thing.

Meantime, downtown stores were feeling the serious effects of the boycott. We started the sit-in demonstrations again while we continued picketing retail stores downtown.

It was never about a hot dog and a Coke!

★ FLORIDA STAR ★

Vol.10-No.59 **And NEWS** Saturday, December 17,1960 -Jacksonville 9, Florida **15 C**

Jax NAACP Youth Council To Continue Counter Sit-ins

Youth Council members Isaac Carnes and Herman Grice picketing Cohen Brothers in the St. James Building, now Jacksonville, Florida City Hall (Courtesy Rodney L. Hurst Sr.)

Business leaders and others brought in Alfred C. Ulmer, a white attorney, to serve as the chair of the committee, and perhaps to play mediator. It really did not matter who chaired the committee. We knew what we wanted to be the committee's final product. As we started sit-ins again, Jacksonville's political structure thought they would wreck the movement, or hamper it as much as possible, with my arrest and with the arrests of Youth Council members. It did not work, and we even stepped up the sit-ins and the picketing while the committee continued to meet.

Mr. Pearson and I attended several committee meetings with Ulmer as chair to discuss our discontent with the process. Fred Schultz, one of the movers and shakers in Jacksonville's business community at the time insisted that Jacksonville's businesses reach an agreement. It was obviously good business sense. I have always felt that in that instance, Fred also thought it was the right thing to do. Finally, after several months of meetings, and numerous back and forth accusations, we reached an agreement that lunch counters in downtown Jacksonville would integrate. The NAACP agreed to the compromise, which mirrored lunch counter integration agreements in other communities in Florida.

Two Blacks would eat at Woolworth's white lunch counter for one week, so whites would become accustomed to Blacks eating there, and, after that week, all downtown lunch counters would integrate. Every day for a week, Marjorie Meeks and I left Edward Waters College between 11:00 a.m. and 11:30 a.m. to eat lunch at the white lunch counter in Woolworth.

We made sure this would not be a situation where Woolworth would bring in a Black waitress just to serve us. We asked for and got assurances that both lunch counters would ultimately integrate.

Eventually the colored lunch counter closed, but before it did, both lunch counters did integrate, and Woolworth did in fact integrate its waitresses at the heretofore-white lunch counter.

Our daily visits that week were quite ordinary and in obvious contrast to our visits the previous summer. The stares were there, and one white waitress refused to serve us, but another white waitress did. James Word, Woolworth's manager, even stopped by to sit and talk with us.

Lunch counters at W. T. Grant, McCrorys, Kress, and Woolworth officially integrated the following week.

At the Youth Council meeting that followed, we did not jump and shout or high-five each other on learning the news that the lunch counters would integrate. We always prayed and asked God for strength and guidance—that his will ultimately would prevail. It helped too that Mr. Pearson fervently believed that God's divine hand would protect us. Several of us led the prayers at that historic Youth Council meeting. During previous Youth Council meetings, I would always alert the person first, that Mr. Pearson, or I would call upon him or her to lead prayers, so they could prepare. Some of us did not pray too well, but we prayed anyway, always acknowledging that God would hear our prayers in the ongoing civil rights struggle.

Though there would be others, we certainly thanked God for this victory.

It was never about a hot dog and a Coke!

REPORT FOR 1961

NAACP
IN
ACTION

NATIONAL ASSOCIATION FOR THE ADVANCEMENT OF COLORED PEOPLE
20 WEST 40TH STREET, NEW YORK 18, NY

The Jacksonville, Fla., youth council under the dynamic leadership of 18-year-old Rodney Hurst, scored one of the major victories of the year when it successfully desegregated all stores in downtown Jacksonville on May 16. This action followed more than ten months of continuous sit-ins and other protest demonstrations conducted by the youth council to force an end to segregation practices within the stores. The consistent action was interruped only once by a brief two-week "cooling-off" period made at the request of the Jacksonville Chamber of Commerce which promised, in turn, to desegregate stores at the termination of the period, provided there was no advance publicity. The council accepted these terms and the stores opened on May 16 as agreed.

*Author's note: I was 16 at the time, not 18.

Chapter 23

Warren Folks

"None of us is responsible for the complexion of his skin. This fact of nature offers no clue to the character or quality of the person underneath."
—Marian Anderson

You could always count on Warren Folks to play the antagonist to both the Black community and to civil rights activities in Jacksonville. An ardent and avowed segregationist, Folks owned a downtown barbershop, which had an ax handle prominently displayed on the wall. Folks called the ax handle "a nigger intimidator." Folks and *Jacksonville Chronicle* publisher Sam Melson were friends. Melson gave Folks a forum in the *Chronicle* and regularly reported on his activities.

In the late fifties, Patrick Henry Saunders, my sister Joan's father and my stepfather, worked as the chief bellman at the Seminole Hotel in downtown Jacksonville. Warren Folks owned or rented a barbershop next to the hotel. Joan calls that period her introduction to bigotry, and related this to me: "Usually on Saturdays, my father would send a taxicab to our house to take me to the Seminole Hotel. One of the members of my daddy's staff would then take me shopping three blocks away at Woolworth. I would notice a man standing outside the barbershop. He just stood and watched the activities at the hotel. I have no idea when he would service his customers, or cut hair, because whenever I went to the Seminole to see my daddy, I would see him standing outside watching. Everyone apparently knew him. When I would get back to the hotel, Daddy would meet me, and I would hug and kiss him, as daughters do. Seeing me hug my daddy appeared to raise the man's blood pressure. I had very fair skin, and from a distance, you could mistake me [for] being white, but you would not mistake my father as white. One day, while again standing in front of the barbershop witnessing me hug and kiss Daddy, the man apparently had enough of this little white girl hugging and kissing a Black male hotel employee, and cursed loud enough for my father and me to hear him. I said, 'Ooh Daddy, that man said a bad word.' My father immediately rushed me into the lobby and I left the hotel a little later.

Several years later, as I stood outside the Seminole Hotel watching a parade, I saw what appeared [to be] a coffin, painted black, on the edge of the sidewalk in front of the barbershop. A hangman's noose dangled above the coffin, and a sign read, 'Martin Luther Coon.' Of course, the man was Warren Folks, standing in front of Folks Barber Shop."

In 1969, I worked for WJCT Channel Seven, the Public Television affiliate in Jacksonville, as a recipient of a Corporation for Public Broadcasting Fellowship to study and work in Public Television. During that period, I co-hosted a public television show called *Feedback*, a nightly live news and public affairs program, which featured guests and an interactive call-in line for viewers. Hurricane Camille, a category 3-4 hurricane, had earlier hit the Gulf Coast, leaving extensive destruction. Richard Brown, the executive director of *Feedback* and the vice president for news and public affairs programming, received a call from Warren Folks asking if he could appear as a guest on *Feedback*. He wanted to discuss his White Cross organization, and his efforts to raise money to help the "white victims" of Hurricane Camille.

We booked guests whose political persuasions covered the philosophical spectrum, so we did not consider an appearance from a segregationist such as Warren Folks out of the ordinary. Nor did the possibility of Folks's appearance bother anyone. Of course, we were all fully aware of Warren Folks's political and social philosophies. This would be his first appearance on *Feedback*, at least since I had started working on the show. He also had another request. He did not want that "Chinese-looking nigger" (guess who?) or any "Jews" to interview him, and he did not talk with guests who were "Jews or niggers." Richard Brown told Warren that the *Feedback* staff and Channel 7 neither condoned nor appreciated that language, and that in addition to him, several members of the *Feedback* staff were Jewish. Folks hung up.

On August 27, 2000, at the program we held at Bethel Baptist Institutional Church to commemorate the fortieth anniversary of Ax Handle Saturday, several civil rights stalwarts and notables attended. They included retired Florida NAACP Field Secretary Robert Saunders, former Florida state senator Arnett Girardeau, humanitarian and conservationist Mavynee

Betsch, former judge and community activist William Maness, civil rights activist and author Stetson Kennedy, C. Ronald Belton, Bethel Baptist senior pastors Reverend Rudolph McKissick Jr. and Reverend Rudolph McKissick Sr., and former Florida State Supreme Court chief justice Leander Shaw, who spoke later that day at another commemorative function.

As I presided at the program, Warren Folks, dressed in camouflage fatigues, walked into Bethel, came up to the church pulpit, extended his hand to shake my hand, and called me his "friend." This was the same Warren Folks who had regularly called Blacks "niggers" and exclaimed how much he hated them; who had referred to Dr. Martin Luther King Jr. as "Martin Luther Coon"; and who proclaimed himself an avowed segregationist. This same Warren Folks asked to shake my hand. I extended my hand to him and shook his.

In this moment of goodwill, whether sincere or not, God had prepared a table in His House "in the presence of mine enemies." What a mighty God we serve!

Warren Folks carrying sign (Courtesy Mary Ann Pearson).

Chapter 24

Summary

"How far you walk in life is determined by your allowing God to walk with you."
            -Rev. Rudolph W. McKissick Sr.

I pray that in the preceding pages you have gained some insight and learned some history about the Jacksonville chapter of the civil rights movement in the late fifties and early sixties.

The civil rights movement in the fifties and the sixties in Jacksonville is a history painted on the human canvas of courage. This book is my eyewitness account to history and our story of historical truth. We have an obligation to tell our story repeatedly until today's generation understands it, embraces it, and internalizes it. Try as some might, you cannot change history or try to soften its impact when the history is unflattering.

Unfortunately, because of intentional news blackouts about the sit-ins and other civil rights activities prior to Ax Handle Saturday, there is not much reference material or photos to review. That is very unfortunate. Still, the Jacksonville community needs to understand the city's racial demeanor during that time in our nation's history.

Ax Handle Saturday is another chapter in the historical testimony of how some preferred to handle the racial situation.

Through the courage of his convictions, Mr. Rutledge Henry Pearson, a schoolteacher, imparted one basic philosophy to his students and the Jacksonville Youth Council NAACP—freedom is not free. If it is worth having, it is worth making a sacrifice and worth fighting the good fight. Despite our youth, we understood that. Blacks in the late fifties and early sixties were not free, and the visible vestiges of segregation proved that.

Because of his involvement with the NAACP Youth Council and the NAACP generally, the Duval County School System's administrators, principals, and athletic directors made Mr. Pearson's life difficult. What he did for Black students in Jacksonville did not make a difference to them.

I visited Mr. Pearson at Isaiah Blocker while home on leave from the Air Force. As I approached his class, I saw Mr. William Harper, the principal of Isaiah Blocker, and Mr. Ish Brant, the superintendent of the Duval County School System, standing outside Mr. Pearson's classroom, listening as he taught his class. Maybe they were digesting a good American History class. Maybe they were confirming Mr. Pearson selection as the,"Teacher of the Year." On the other hand, maybe, just maybe, they were hoping to hear something they could use against him.

After I told Mr. Pearson he had guests in the hall listening to his class, he smiled and continued teaching his class in true Rutledge Pearson style. In teaching American History, he refused to compromise his beliefs, especially the importance of contributions made by Blacks. Mr. Pearson later introduced me to the class and told them about my involvement in the sit-ins and the Youth Council NAACP. It felt like old times.

During those years of segregation, Duval County School system administrators certainly intimidated many a Black schoolteacher. But unprofessionally hovering outside his classroom door, listening to his teaching an all-inclusive history of this country, did not intimidate Mr. Pearson.

Though Superintendent Brant and his subordinates continually tried to find charges to press against him, Mr. Pearson did not change his teaching style, the content of the courses he taught, nor his civil rights message to assuage his would-be professional detractors.

In 1964, now the President of the Florida State Conference of NAACP Branches and a member of the Board of Directors of the National NAACP, Duval County School officials blamed Mr. Pearson, in part, for a walkout by Black teachers and Black students. Superintendent Ish Brant, and Negro Superintendent Dr. John Irving Elias Scott, even directed several Black school system high school and junior high school officials to corroborate their findings and fire Mr. Pearson as the New Stanton High School baseball coach. These included Isaiah Blocker Junior High School Principal William Harper, New Stanton

Senior High School Principal Charles D. Brooks, and New Stanton Senior High School Athletic Director James P. Small. Being the president of the Jacksonville Branch NAACP and president of the Florida State Conference of Branches NAACP obviously helped them orchestrate their blame-game against Mr. Pearson, which relieved both superintendents of responsibility. Some reasoned they were just doing their jobs. Others in the community were not as kind, and publicly called them other names I will not mention. Courage for some is a badge of accomplishment; for others, it is something from which you run. Unfortunately, Mr. Pearson would leave the Duval County School System to work for International Laundry Worker's Union.

Not surprisingly, we still discuss issues today that we discussed in the fifties and the sixties: a lack of communication between whites and Blacks, the politics of exclusion and segregation, the politics of slavery, violence against Blacks, mostly Black schools having to suffer from inadequate capital outlay and operational resources, problems between the community and the police department; affirmative action, or the lack thereof, and of course, racism. I guess the adage still applies— the more things change, the more they remain the same. Many Blacks today appear indifferent to these issues, while many whites still do not want to discuss them.

When February rolls around every year, we roll out the same tired, comfortable, and non-threatening exhibits of Black history. In fact, some schools do not change or update their Black history exhibits. They simply dust them off and put them up. Most Black and white students consider Black history a novelty. To them, Black history happens during a single month, and after that, it is back to real American History, with little or no discussion of the relevant contributions by Black Americans. One would interpret that to mean that this generation does not respect Black history. Even the staid and archaic world of public education should right that wrong.

In today's society, Black and white Americans must realize the important, rich legacy of the civil rights movement, and the struggle for human dignity and respect. There are those who feel the civil rights struggle is over. Certainly, there are no visual signs that exclaim "COLORED WAITING ROOMS" or "COLORED LUNCH COUNTERS" or "COLORED WATER FOUNTAINS." As a Black young lady said to me, we can go everywhere we want and do everything we want.

Because you cannot see the visible vestiges of racism and segregation does not mean that racism and segregation no longer exist. Fighting for civil rights today requires the same diligence as it did in the sixties. Believe me, there is still a war to fight. If we are committed to meaningful race relations in Jacksonville, we must have serious dialogue and communication between the white community and the Black community.

I have lived in Jacksonville all of my life and at times, race relations studies amuse me. Every time you survey Blacks in Jacksonville and ask them to document the problems and the impact of discriminatory practices and racism, they give you countless examples. Racial profiling, job discrimination, first fired at times of downsizing, woefully inadequate support and resources for schools located in the Black community, lack of infrastructure improvements in the community— the list is long, and supporting documents can be stacked from floor to ceiling. Of course, after completion, such studies usually go on the shelf, with weak promises to address the problems.

You can compare every racial study completed in Jacksonville over the years, and find that the results are remarkably similar; which means the problems have not changed and this community has not addressed them. Blacks know that racial studies done in Jacksonville have provided few positive results, and usually only benefit the paid consultants. Despite their good intentions, a few study groups here and there will not solve the problems. They will never succeed until there is an action resolve to make real and substantive changes.

Many years ago, members of the Jacksonville Youth Council NAACP understood the fight and the struggle. Following the lead of a courageous young Black schoolteacher, they fought to right some of the wrongs of racism and segregation in the Jacksonville community. Such fights are never easy, but you base your fight on the courage of your convictions.

If Jacksonville is to reach a level of greatness, men and women of good will must continually attack racism at every level. The consequences should not be a consideration.

Chapter 25

Mr. Pearson's Death

"Freedom is never given; it is won."
—A. Philip Randolph

In the early afternoon of May 1, 1967, I received a frantic call from my wife Ann. I had spent several days at home, recuperating from a spring virus and severe pharyngitis. Ann and I had gotten married almost five months earlier.

We were to move into our new house in Washington Heights around the middle of December, but due to construction delays, we did not move in until late December 1966. While we waited, our good friends, Roberta and Kenneth Manual, let us stay in their apartment (our honeymoon cottage) for several days while they attended to Kenneth's ill mother.

We came home one day to find, in our new residence, an ironing board and an iron on our porch—wedding gifts from Mr. and Mrs. Pearson. When I got inside, I called Mr. Pearson to thank him for the wedding gifts. He explained that he would have brought it to the wedding earlier in the month, but added, "I could see the headlines now: 'State NAACP President Drags Ironing Board Wedding Gift Up Church Stairs During Wedding.'" We laughed about how the press would have treated that "news story." He decided to wait to deliver it in person.

Ann began telling me something that sounded so unreal it's hard to believe, even today. She tried to make her words as painless to me as possible, but they still crushed me, "Rodney, Mr. Pearson was killed in an automobile accident in Tennessee." After being forced out of the Duval County school system, Mr. Pearson went to work for the International Laundry Workers Union as a union organizer. He had gone to Tennessee a few days earlier on union business. Ann's words had a hollow sound to them.

There is no cushion for news like that. News of the death of a friend or family member always stabs—quick, deep, and painful. Dealing with the pain of death is such an indescribable pain, as is the painful death of a great friend and "family member." Mr. Pearson was both of those to me and many others. I sat down and stared.

I do not think I asked her where or how Mr. Pearson was killed or when it happened. Ann would tell me later that I asked, and she said her manager (at the Federal Reserve Bank) heard it on the news.

When I went completely blank on the phone, Ann asked if I was all right. She asked me if she needed to come home.

My eyes caught the iron and the ironing board, which were still up from earlier that morning. I told her I would be all right. I immediately called the NAACP office. NAACP office secretary Allie Faye Maxwell Polite tearfully confirmed the news. When she received the initial call from Tennessee about Mr. Pearson's death, she screamed and threw the phone down, she would later tell me. I called Jacksonville pediatrician and NAACP stalwart Dr. C. B. McIntosh, who also confirmed Mr. Pearson's death.

For the first time in my life, I cried unashamedly, and I did not care who heard or saw as I sat home alone.

I have since heard learned theologians like my former priest, the late Father Sidney Parker at St. Gabriel Episcopal Church, and my current Pastors, Reverend Rudolph McKissick Sr. and Reverend Rudolph McKissick Jr., preach great eulogies that would give spiritual comfort to grieving families. I could have used one of those eulogies. I had no one to talk with at that moment to ease my pain.

I was twenty-three, had spent four years in the Air Force, and was married, but I could have been sixteen and Youth Council NAACP president again. I had flashbacks that chronicled great NAACP moments spent with Mr. Pearson and the Jacksonville Youth Council NAACP: moments spent as mentor and mentee; as big brother and little brother; as father and son; as teacher and student; as advisor and advisee; as friends; traveling with the Youth Council members to Virginia, North Carolina, South Carolina, Georgia, and Miami, Florida; and as I really paused to think about it, as civil rights fighters. I think that was the first time I thought of myself as a civil rights fighter.

My phone started to ring. I did not want to talk to anyone. Friends and neighbors were getting home from work. We were a close-knit community in Washington Heights, where a number of young married couples lived. Several friends and neighbors came by, but I simply did not feel like talking to anyone.

When Ann got home, she helped console me as much as she could and as much as I would let her, but my pity-party was in full gear. I was not very pleasant that day or for several days to follow.

I remembered reading an article in *Jet* magazine in 1964 that featured Mr. Pearson on the cover.

JET Cover

In the article, a reporter wrote, "He can wheel and deal with every segment. He holds this Negro town together. If he is killed, let's hope it'll be in an auto accident." I had a quick negative flashback to that article, and wondered if Mr. Pearson's death resulted from an automobile accident, or if racist elements had once again been successful in silencing another strong Black male voice in the movement.

The location of Mr. Pearson's funeral services became an issue because we in the NAACP knew, as did Mrs. Pearson and the Pearson family, that people would attend Mr. Pearson's funeral from all across the country.

We made a conscious decision to request the use of Shiloh Metropolitan Baptist Church. We asked Reverend Coleman to hold Mr. Pearson's funeral there because it was still the largest Black church in Jacksonville. Reverend Coleman agreed, but as he and Shiloh did with the Jackie Robinson mass meeting, Reverend Coleman and Shiloh charged the NAACP and Mrs. Pearson $100 for use of the church— simply an amazing repeat of what they did with the NAACP mass meeting ten years earlier with circumstances this time more serious.

What a tremendous opportunity to right a previous wrong and acknowledge the greatness of this civil rights hero who would soon lie in state in the sanctuary of your church. Regrettably, Reverend Coleman and Shiloh did not understand and it appeared useless to make him understand. In some situations and issues, you pray over, and try to forgive but not forget. This was one of those "not forget" instances for me.

Of course, people did come from around the country to pay homage and respect to another fallen civil rights fighter.

My mind will not let me remember a lot about the days following Mr. Pearson's death and the days leading to his funeral, yet some events and images remain vivid.

- I remember Earl Johnson literally wailing outside Mr. Pearson's house, either the night of his death or the next night.
- I remember thinking that Mrs. Pearson would have to raise Pat, Bud, and Roderick (their children) by herself.

It was never about a hot dog and a Coke!

IN MEMORIAM

OF THE LATE

RUTLEDGE H. PEARSON, SR.

SATURDAY, MAY 6, 1967   3:00 P.M.

SHILOH METROPOLITAN BAPTIST CHURCH

INTERMENT IN EVERGREEN CEMETERY

by

HOLMES AND WEST FUNERAL HOME

- I remember Allie Faye Maxwell Polite's voice melodiously wafting to the rafters of the church as she sang one of Mr. Pearson's favorite songs, "I'll Walk with God."
- I remember thinking that Allie Faye, six months earlier, had sung at my wedding to Ann.
- I remember the remaining three members of the renowned Huston-Tillotson Quartet—Mr. Pearson had sung baritone—in their quartet

singing formation, an open space where Mr. Pearson would have stood.

TILLOTSON COLLEGE QUARTET

(Courtesy Mary Ann Pearson).

- I remember Quartet members Andrew Day, Walter Anders and Nathaniel Greene singing the Lord's Prayer in glorious three-part harmony, with the baritone part unsung. (I often wondered how they would have sounded with Mr. Pearson.)
- I remember sitting next to Ulysses Beatty in Shiloh and discussing how difficult it would be carrying Mr. Pearson's casket as pallbearers.
- I remember Earl Johnson opening his remarks at the funeral with, "Rutledge, I cry no more."
- I remember trying my best not to cry at the church—public male machismo, I guess—and losing that battle badly.
- I remember thinking that Mr. Pearson would still be alive if some Blacks and whites had not forced him out of the Duval County School System.

I have kept a copy of Mr. Pearson's funeral program for 40 years. By most accounts, Mr. Pearson's funeral cortege was the city's longest at that time.

There were also some ironic firsts in the aftermath of Mr. Pearson's death:

- The *Florida Times-Union* discontinued "News For and About the Colored People of Jacksonville" later in 1967. *Their official explanation?* "It is time."
- The first pictures of Black brides (not by design) to appear on the heretofore white brides' pages of the *Florida Times-Union* and in the "regular" newspaper were those of his brother Lloyd's beautiful daughters, Delores Pearson Baker (Robert) and Barbara Pearson McCreary (Richard).
- Mr. Pearson was the first Black buried in previously segregated Evergreen Cemetery on Main Street in Jacksonville.
- After my election to the Jacksonville City Council in 1975, one of my first legislative accomplishments was naming the bridge on Moncrief Road (in Jacksonville, Florida) Rutledge Henry Pearson Bridge.
- An elementary school in the Duval County School System also bears his name.

While doing the research for this book and talking with Mrs. Pearson, we both questioned some issues related to Mr. Pearson's death that we had never discussed with each other before.

Mrs. Pearson never saw a copy of a medical examiners' report from Waynesboro, Tennessee, where the accident took place. No one told her the kind of injury and the extent of the injury that caused Mr. Pearson's death. And she never saw an autopsy report.

I have tried not to dwell on my feelings, and have probably suppressed many mental deliberations, about how Mr. Pearson died. I certainly cannot shake the comment from the reporter in that *Jet* magazine article. But when you understand what this country is capable of doing, and allowed to be done to civil rights fighters—how elements of American society are encouraged to respond negatively and violently to civil rights—I don't believe for one moment that Mr. Pearson died the way the official account or the accident report states he died.

Mrs. Pearson does not believe the official account either.

40th Commemorative Anniversary Program of Ax Handle Saturday - from left, former State Senator Arnett E. Girardeau; Rodney L. Hurst Sr.; former State Supreme Court Chief Justice Leander Shaw; civil rights activist Stetson Kennedy; Alton Yates; and former Jacksonville Judge Bill Maness.

It is worth noting that a civil rights marker now stands in Hemming Park, in downtown Jacksonville, attesting to the historical importance of Ax Handle Saturday, and to the courage of the Jacksonville Youth Council NAACP and its advisor, Rutledge Henry Pearson.

At least in this instance, Jacksonville finally got it right.

Jacksonville Youth Council NAACP
Hall of Fame 1960

(I have listed Youth Council members in alphabetical order by their first name. Their married name is in parenthesis.)

ALTON YATES (Youth Council NAACP 1st Vice President) is the vice president of development of OTAI, and holds a masters degree in public administration (urban studies). He retired from the Air Force after 32 years. He is a Ford Foundation/Yale University Graduate National Urban Fellow. An ardent proponent of logistics, business process management, and systems dynamics, Mr. Yates operated the U.S. Army's Vehicle Maintenance Facility at the Pine Bluff Arsenal. He served as administrative aide to four mayoral administrations in the City of Jacksonville and as the director of the regulatory and environmental services department of the City of Jacksonville. Mr. Yates joined OTAI (Over the Air Institute) Technologies, a systems integration and technology services provider in 2000 as vice president of corporate development. He leverages his wealth of knowledge of the public and private sectors by broadening OTAI market initiatives.

Arnett Girardeau
(Courtesy Florida Photographic Collection)

ARNETT GIRARDEAU (Captain of Ax Handle Saturday sit-in demonstration) received his undergraduate degree from Howard

University and graduated from the Howard University College of Dentistry. Elected to the Florida House of Representatives in 1976, he served three two-year terms before becoming the first Black male elected to the Florida Senate in 1982. His great-uncle, Richard L. Brown, was the last Black from Jacksonville, to serve in the Florida Legislature during reconstruction (1881-1883). Later, he would become the first Black elected (by his fellow Florida State Senators) to serve as President Pro Tempore of the Florida Senate. Dr. Girardeau continues to involve himself in issues, which affect the Black community specifically, and the Jacksonville community generally.

Earl Johnson (Courtesy Jacksonville, Florida City Council Archives).

EARL JOHNSON (Jacksonville NAACP Legal Counsel) Earl Johnson received his law degree from Howard University. He served five years in the Army including a tour of duty as an Infantry lieutenant. A native of West Virginia, he moved to Jacksonville in 1957 entering into law practice with Leander Shaw. Earl served as Chief NAACP Legal Counsel for the Jacksonville Branch NAACP and the Florida Conference of Branches NAACP. During the St. Augustine, Florida racial riots in 1964, he represented Dr. Robert Hayling and Dr. Martin Luther King in federal court. He was the first Black elected to an at-large seat on the consolidated Jacksonville City Council serving 15 years from 1967 – 1983; and, the first Black voted by fellow Jacksonville City Council members to serve as City Council President.

HENRY L. GARDNER (Youth Council NAACP Treasurer) is managing partner of Gardner, Underwood, and Bacon, a municipal management-consulting firm he established in 1995. He previously served as senior vice president of Donaldson, Luftkin & Jennette Securities Corporation and city manager of Oakland, California, where he began his career as an assistant personnel analyst in 1971. He serves on numerous boards of directors and is past president of the National Forum for Black Public Administrators. He has a Bachelor of Arts degree in political science and speech from the University of Illinois at Urbana-Champaign and a Masters of Arts degree in government from Southern Illinois University at Carbondale.

MARJORIE MEEKS (BROWN) (Youth Council NAACP Secretary) made history as the first female postmaster of Atlanta, Georgia on November 9, 1996, leading a team of 33 managers and directing the efforts of more than 2,400 employees, with responsibility for annual revenues exceeding $614 million. Prior to her appointment as postmaster of Atlanta, she served as district manager for the Westchester District in White Plains, New York. A manager for 30 of her 38 years in the postal service, Ms. Brown held executive positions as director, marketing & communications and as manager, retail sales and service in Miami, Orlando, and Jacksonville, Florida. Ms. Brown attended Edward Waters College and completed management studies at Duke University, Emory University, and the University of Virginia, and is a graduate of 2001 Leadership Atlanta. She takes great pride as the mother of five adult children and the grandmother of seven.

Leander Shaw (Courtesy Florida Photographic Collection).

LEANDER SHAW (Jacksonville NAACP Assistant Legal Counsel) earned his juris doctor degree in 1957 from Howard University in

Washington, D.C. Attorney Shaw taught as an assistant professor of law at Florida A&M University in 1957. Admitted to the Florida Bar in 1960, he went into private practice in Jacksonville with Earl Johnson, and served as assistant public defender. In 1974, Governor Reubin Askew appointed him to the Florida Industrial Relations Commission, where he served until October 1979, when Governor Bob Graham appointed him to the First District Court of Appeal. In January 1983, Governor Graham appointed him to the Supreme Court, where he served as Chief Justice from 1990 to 1992. He retired from the State Supreme Court in 2002.

Youth Council Members

Alphonso Stanfield
Ann Bradley
Annie Albertie (Hurst)
Annie Lou Johnson
Barbara Hilliard
Barbara Pearson (McCrary)
Barbara Simmons (Van Blake)
  [deceased]
Betty Harper
Bill Holton
Carolyn Graham
Carstairs Robinson
Colbert Britt
Delores Pearson (Baker)
Gene Stinson [deceased]
George Tutson [deceased]
Gwen Garner (Yates)
Hazel Yates
Helen Britt
Herman Grice
Iona Godfrey
Isaac Carnes

Jacqueline Stephens (Phelts)
James Rapley
Joan Holzendorf [deceased]
Kent Pearson
Leroy Bass
Linda Malpress
Lloyd Pearson III
Margaret Bradley
Mary Alice King
McKinley Genwright [deceased]
Nina Ann Stone
Paulette Malpress [deceased]
Quillie Jones
Richard West
Robert Butts
Roderick Freeman [deceased]
Rodney L. Hurst
Ronald Stephens
Rometa Graham (Porter)
Rose Ann Shine
Sylvia Tyson
Sonja Mathews (Sprott)

Once to ev'ry man and nation,
Comes the moment to decide,
Then it is the brave man and woman who chooses,
While the coward stands aside,
Doubting in his abject spirit,
'Til his very Lord is crucified.
—from Once to Ev'ry Man and Nation
by James Lowell

About the Author

Acknowledged as a community activist at an early age, Rodney Hurst joined the Jacksonville Youth Council NAACP at the invitation of Rutledge Pearson, the Youth Council's advisor. He was eleven. The uniqueness about his joining was that Pearson was also Hurst's eighth grade American History teacher and the invitation came in the classroom. Hurst considers meeting Rutledge Pearson and subsequently joining the NAACP as having one of the greatest impacts on his life.

Born in Jacksonville in 1944, Hurst later became President of the Jacksonville Youth Council NAACP in 1959, and led the Youth Council's sit-in demonstrations in the summer of 1960. Those demonstrations culminated in the now infamous "Ax Handle Saturday" when 200 segregationists with ax handles and baseball bats, attacked 35 members of the Jacksonville Youth Council NAACP, in downtown Jacksonville. Though lunch counter sit-in and other demonstrations were very visible in 1960, Mr. Hurst is quick to point out that demonstrations were about "…human dignity and respect. Lunch counters were just visible and convenient venues to attack racial discrimination."

Hurst is the recipient of numerous recognitions and awards. He is a member of the Bethel Baptist Institutional Church where he actively serves in the Fine Arts Ministry. He and his wife Ann have been married for 41 years. They have two sons, Todd, and Rodney (Danita), and two granddaughters Marquiette, and Jasmine. His hobbies are Oldies and Motown music, and he spends what he calls quality time, as an "Oldies" DJ.

To Form a More Perfect Union

No one interpretive picture captures the totality and the struggle of the civil rights movement like this grouping of sculptures created by Studio EIS of Brooklyn, New York.

From NAACP picket lines, to responsible and not so responsible media, to police in gas masks, to National Guard members in full riot gear and drawn rifles, to the image of Rosa Parks, and finally, lunch counter sit-ins complete with taunting crowd.

The two seated figures on the right of the lunch counter were the images used representing lunch counter sit-ins in the United States Postal Service 2005 Civil Rights Commemorative Stamp Issue, "To Form a More Perfect Union".

Index

Payne, Willard 107
Pearson, Mary Ann v, 36, 47, 169, 172, 175, 176
Pearson, Rutledge Henry v, xi, 12, 28, 29, 30, 31, 32, 33, 34, 35, 36, 37, 38, 39, 40, 41, 45, 46, 47, 48, 49, 50, 51, 55, 57, 66, 69, 70, 71, 77, 81, 84, 86, 90, 91, 92, 103, 104, 120, 122, 123, 128, 130, 131, 134, 136, 150, 152, 153, 156, 157, 158, 159, 160, 165, 166, 167, 169, 170, 171, 172, 173, 174, 175
Penn Center 148, 149, 150
Pittsburgh Courier 20, 134

R

Reynolds, Luther 95, 99
Richmond, Virginia 150, 151
Robinson, Jackie 19, 29, 43, 44, 45, 172
Rothschild, Arv 33

S

Sanders, Robert W. 120
Satterwhite, Dr. Hunter 33
Saunders, Janelle 2
Saunders, Bob 39, 84, 86, 90, 92
Santora, Judge John 98, 99
Schell, Dr. W. W. 33
Schultz, Fred 156, 159
Scott, John Irving Elias 9
Sears, Clarence 75, 76
Shaw, Leander 127, 164
Shiloh Metropolitan Baptist Church 43, 172
Silverman, Sol 91, 93
Simpson, Eric 59, 92, 114, 129
Simpson, Caledonia 12
Small, James P. 167
Smith, Mildred 84
Sprinkle, Iva T. 10
St. Helena Islands 148, 149

Stallings, State Representative George B. Jr. 145
Stephens, Jacqueline 106, 181
Stewart, William 125
Sumpter, Bernell 22
Sutton, Charles 'Knots' 22

T

Thompson, Camilla 12
Thompson, Charles "Tree Top" 22
Tutson, George 59, 181
Two Spot 17, 18
Twiggs, Lila 5

U

U. S. Civil Rights Commission 91
Unitarian Universalist Church 121
United States Supreme Court 11

W

W. T. Grant Department store 57, 71, 72
Walker, Billy "Bowlegs" 22
Walton, Julian "Bill" 22
Warren, Chief Justice Earl 10
Washington, Dr. Emmitt 33
West Jacksonville Elementary School 2
Westside Widow's Club 6
White, Dr. Alvin G. 22
Wilder Park 22, 69
Wilder Recreation Park Center 69
Wiles, Very 13
Wilkins, Roy 39, 84, 86, 112, 113, 114, 148, 151, 152
Williams, Lizzie Foreman 2
Williams, I. E. "Mama" 75
Wilson, Rev. Robert H. 41
Woodson, Carter G. 27
Woolworth Department Store 52, 53, 54, 55, 57, 58, 59, 65, 66, 67, 71, 72, 89, 94, 160, 162

Word, James 59, 89, 160
Wylie, Ralph 23

Y

Yates, Alton 51, 58, 59, 60, 86, 92, 106, 120, 134, 136, 153, 176
Youth Center 51, 57, 62, 64, 67, 70, 75, 77, 81

LaVergne, TN USA
11 September 2009
157443LV00005B/31/P